'Like imagining a shark chasing you while doing laps in the pool. After reading the first few chapters of *I Ran for My Life*, Mabalane's new tell-all book, and coming to grips with how deep his struggle with drugs and depression have been over the past 20 years, I assume that for him it was his past that he was running away from. But it's much more than that.'
– Garreth van Niekerk, *City Press*

'Mabalane's insecurities are laid bare in the book. It was these insecurities, he recounts, that led him to drugs and booze. Drugs aside, this is also a book about redemption and salvation, perhaps where the phrase "I ran for my life" comes into play. Mabalane portrays jogging as his saving grace. It was a starting point in his regeneration tale.'
– *Business Day*

'*I Ran for My Life* cleverly uses a guide on how to run the Comrades Marathon and juxtaposes that with the good, the bad and the ugly of [Kabelo's] life so far ...'
– Helen Herimaba, *The Star*

'Kabelo details how a drug and alcohol addiction led him to almost lose everything he had worked for. After going through rehab he gained weight, so he started running. Little did he realise running would be such a large part of his recovery.'
– *The Citizen*

To Gail, thank you for your unrelenting support

I Ran For My Life

My Story

Kabelo Mabalane

with Nechama Brodie

MACMILLAN

First published in 2015
by Pan Macmillan South Africa

This edition published in 2016
by Pan Macmillan South Africa
Private Bag X19
Northlands
Johannesburg
2116

www.panmacmillan.co.za

ISBN 978-1-77010-499-0

© 2015, 2016 Kabelo Mabalane

All rights reserved. No part of this publication
may be reproduced, stored in or introduced into a
retrieval system, or transmitted, in any form or by
any means (electronic, mechanical, photocopying,
recording or otherwise), without the prior written
permission of the publisher. Any person who does
any unauthorised act in relation to this publication
may be liable to criminal prosecution and civil
claims for damages.

Editing by Kelly Norwood-Young
Proofreading by Wesley Thompson
Design and typesetting by Triple M
Cover design by K4
Front cover photograph by Chris Saunders
Back cover photograph by Kevin Mark Pass

Printed and bound by Shumani Mills Communications, Parow, Cape Town
SW61044

Contents

Up 1
Soweto, 1976 3
The Hills in Your Mind 14
You Must Always Fight Back 15
Letting Go of a Situation Doesn't Mean Letting Go of Who You Are 25
Make the 'Big Picture' Simple 38
Music was My Last Resort 40
Tokollo, Kabelo and Zwai, aka TKZee 46
The Platinum-Selling Failure 52
Between the Start and the Finish 58
There is Always Something to be Grateful For 59
Endings and Interventions 68
Solo to Sober 75
The Hill without End 87
I am the Monster 88
The Beat Goes On 99
A Rock and Roll Singer Who Loves Jesus Christ 109
Conversations with Myself 116
My Big Belly Day 118
Everything and Nothing to Prove 131
Faith Records 138
You Have to Forget Past Victories 142

Ten Minutes Too Early 149
I've Got to be that Guy 155

Run, Eat, Live: A Guide from 0–89 Kilometres 159
The Start Line 161
Ross Tucker's 12-Week, 10-Kilometre Programme 166
Running a Half-Marathon 169
Ross Tucker's Nine-Week, Half-Marathon Programme 171
Marathons and Ultramarathons 178
Ross Tucker's 10-Week Marathon and Ultramarathon
    Programme 181
How to Run the Comrades Marathon 188
Nutrition 198
Running Safety and Etiquette 211
Kabelo's Top Running Playlist 216

Acknowledgements 217

Up

One thing I hate about the Comrades Marathon is that the distance markers never tell you how far you have run. They always tell you how far you still have to go.

The 'up' run starts at the Durban City Hall and ends, some 87 kilometres later, at the Oval Cricket Stadium in Pietermaritzburg. The 'down' run goes the other way around, from Pietermaritzburg to Durban, finishing off at the Kingsmead Cricket Stadium. The actual distance varies each year depending on the final route, alternating between 'up' and 'down', but the course is somewhere between 86.9 kilometres and 90 kilometres. It's FAR. Like driving from Johannesburg to Sasolburg, or from Cape Town to Bot River. Except you don't have a car. All you have is two feet, two legs, and a mind that, you hope, keeps telling you to put one foot in front of the other and not stop doing that.

I ran my first Comrades Marathon in 2006, three and a half years after I came out of rehab for cocaine and alcohol addiction. The race took me nearly 11 hours to finish. It was maybe the hardest thing I had ever done, but it was also one of my biggest achievements. I was already a best-selling musician – TKZee still holds the record for the fastest-selling single by a South African artist, and I had three double-platinum solo albums under my belt. But when I ran Comrades, it was something else. I finally proved, to everyone (and maybe to myself), that I was a finisher.

By the time I ran my seventh Comrades, in 2013, my time was closing in on eight hours, putting me in the top 10–15% of the 18 000-plus runners who take part each year (on anniversary years, there can be up to 23 000 runners). My goal, now, is to run fast enough to get a silver medal, to finish the race in less than seven and a half hours. I haven't made it yet, but I don't plan on giving up.

When you run a race like the Comrades Marathon, you are supposed to have a Plan (with a capital P). I've never had a plan – and I envy the runners who do. For a big race you are also supposed to have 'milestones'. I always find that too nerve-wracking. If you don't reach these milestones then, mentally, you're stuffed – and you never recover. For me, it is all about what happens on the day. That doesn't mean I don't have a strategy. The only way you can *not* have a plan and finish the race is to make sure you still train and prepare. It's the preparation that allows you not to have a plan. Because then you are prepared for anything.

At the start of the Comrades Marathon, I am generally pretty relaxed. I go through the route in my mind, double-check that everything is organised – my shakes and my supplements. For some reason I always have an urgent need to go to the bathroom before the start, so I make sure I've gone for a leak. That is about as close as I get to anything like a ritual. What I focus on, what is more important, is where my head is at. I ask myself whether the goal I'm about to reach for is attainable, whether I am really going to make it.

Also, I make my mind up about finishing, regardless of what happens on the day. It is not an option not to finish.

Soweto, 1976

> *I have this one memory of my mom, my dad, and me, sitting on the patch of lawn outside our house in Pimville. I must have been three, maybe four years old. Before my brother was born. It was afternoon – there was almost like a picnic vibe – and I could just feel the connection between the three of us. In my mind I was having a total blast; I was really happy. There are many things from my childhood that I think I remember quite vividly. But when I try to recall them in detail, I realise they are often memories constructed in hindsight, or from photographs. Sometimes I think I dreamed that day, at our house, because my parents' relationship became very volatile at times. It feels like there's a big chunk of my own life that I missed out on, or that I don't really know.*

My dad always used to say – after he'd had a few drinks – that I had made him a man. I have this image of me being born, and my dad having to get his act together.

My father was born in Sophiatown, and came to Meadowlands with his family after they were forcibly removed. My mom had grown up in Soweto, and her family all lived there. My parents met at a music concert in late 1974, The Staple Singers were performing. My mom says she refused to speak to my dad at first, but he managed to track her down in Diepkloof. She worked as a teacher at Progress High School in Pimville and my dad worked in the underwriting department at Liberty Life in town. After my parents got married they lived in Meadowlands, with my uncle and aunt, before they moved to their own house in a new section in Pimville called New Homes Pimville Z/2.

In Pimville we were a stone's throw away from the main road, but when I was a kid the streets were pretty empty. We would play, ride our bikes. There was a game we called Chicago, where we used to build up these towers out of empty tins. We would make a stack of them, with the Frisco coffee can at the bottom, then a jam can, and so on, from the biggest to the smallest, with the baked bean cans at the top. And then we would have to stand maybe 20 metres away, behind some line, and throw a tennis ball at the tower until it was knocked over, at which point that team would have to run and try rebuild it as fast as they could, while the other team tried to get them out by throwing the tennis ball at them instead of at the cans. We would shout 'Chicago' either after we'd knocked the tins over, or after we'd finished building. We also played Black Mampatile, which was like hide-and-go-seek. Some of the games involved nursery rhymes, which I absolutely loved because it was all about the rhythm – the rhythm was everything! *Tsamo reka Omo. OMO!* We could play that for hours. We would start with the beginning part, but then there was another whole section, and it got harder and harder as it went along. And if we made a mistake we had to start all over again.

Our house had a grass area at the front, and a mini driveway, and more grass at the back where the washing line was. My dad didn't drive until much later in his life so my mom used to drive him everywhere in her Toyota Corolla, or he would catch public transport. This was just my dad's way of doing things. I wouldn't say he was anti-establishment, but he just did things his own way. Nothing fussed him. Once he won a car in a competition and he sold it so he could take the money instead. I don't know if he even bothered getting his licence later. He just decided it was time to start driving, and then he drove.

The house in Pimville wasn't a big house: there was my parents' bedroom, which connected to the bathroom. There was a kitchen, and a lounge where we watched TV and ate our meals. Then there was my bedroom. *Our* bedroom, when my brother came along in 1980.

I don't really have any memories of my brother as a baby, although I've seen photographs of the two of us together. It was different when my little sister was born, in 1987. By then I was nearly 11 years old, and I have very clear recollections. Not of my mom being pregnant – at that stage pregnancy was a very foreign concept to me. I didn't know about pregnancy like I do now, now that I have my own child! If you had said to me that a kid fell from the sky, I think I would have believed it. But I remember there being a tiny baby in our house. Once I sneaked into my mom's bedroom where the baby was sleeping, and just looked at her, stared at this person for the longest time. There was a definite feeling of love, and warmth. The fact that it was a girl made it warmer. I was always very proud to have a little sister – we've had that 'big brother-little sister' thing our whole lives. There's even a certain voice she puts on when she talks to me. With my brother it's always been more volatile. One minute we would be sharing everything, next thing we would be fighting. It's like that today. He was the best man at my white wedding. Then, at my traditional wedding, we had a massive argument. We're still learning how to deal with each other.

My brother didn't stay at home with us at the beginning. For about six or nine months, when he was a baby, he went to live with my paternal grandparents in Rustenburg. I had a different arrangement: my parents sent me to stay with my mom's mother, who lived in Diepkloof. I would stay there from Monday to Friday, when my mom would pick me up; then she would drop me off again on Sunday night. It's not something that was ever discussed with us, but obviously there was a lot of pressure, with both of my parents having to work, and having two small kids. And my mom was always studying, trying to further her education. My mother holds a teacher's diploma. She was also trying to get her BA degree at Unisa, but she never managed to finish it. One of her courses at Unisa was library science. She said there was no point in finishing it anyway, because blacks were not allowed at the National Library in Pretoria. Later she did a diploma in school librarianship with the Soweto College of Education.

My maternal gran's name was Priscilla Matlakala Montsitsi. I would call her Nkgono, or Ma. Eventually I started calling her Ma. My gran was very old-school in her thinking, very tribal. She always used to tell me: 'Don't you marry a Zula woman.' She used to say Zula, not Zulu.

She lived with my granddad, 'Tate Kgolo. He was usually at work during the day, only coming back at night, and I didn't see as much of him; but he was a legend in his own right. I always thought of my granddad as being a very strong man. He was physically strong – he would walk everywhere, and he did karate. But he also commanded respect. I wouldn't say he was aloof, but he came from that generation where 'men were men'. And he was independent; he was always doing his own thing. He worked at Philips, the electronics company, and he could drive. He had a VW Beetle. I had huge respect for him, also because my mom adored my granddad. When she would speak about him, you could always hear that love just in her tone of voice.

My gran's house in Diepkloof was also four rooms. My mother's brothers were still living at home, and they shared the one bedroom. When I lived there, or when I used to stay over, I would sleep in the same room as my gran and granddad. My gran used to make a bed for me at the side of her bed – it wasn't even a mattress, just blankets on top of blankets on top of blankets. And when I would wake up in the morning she would have made *ting* – sour pap – for breakfast.

All my best childhood food was cooked by my gran. Her tripe and samp, and *ting* porridge for breakfast or as a starch at night. My mom used to make *ting* as well, but it wasn't the same. When I would go to gran's house she would always ask what I wanted, and I would say *mogodu*, and then she would go off to the market and she would cook the whole day, and when night-time came, praise God. I guess my mom didn't have the same time. She was obviously working all day, and tripe takes too long. My gran had time to simmer.

I pretty much got whatever I wanted when I was at my gran's. I could laze around the whole day, watch TV. I think we were one of the first houses in Diepkloof to get a television – I guess we got one because my granddad worked at Philips – and all these people used to come watch at Gran's house. Gran would sit at the back, on her chair, and the rest of us would be on the floor, under the table, completely glued to whatever we were watching. I remember us being silent, but eventually my gran would get *gatvol* and she would kick everybody out and tell them to go home. We also used to have a video machine, and we would record the shows we liked. Luckily my uncles loved music. I remember seeing the video for Michael Jackson's 'Beat It' with them.

I went to nursery school in Diepkloof, somewhere in Zone 4. The school is still there – it even looks the same: very kid-friendly, with two patches of green grass in the front, and a fence that allows you to see through to the street. There are slides and see-saws, a jungle gym in all those playground colours: red, green, blue, yellow. I just remember sleeping a lot when I was there. In the afternoons, my gran would pick me up and we would walk back to her house.

In 1982 I started at Ikaneng Primary School, in what we used to call Sub A. I suppose everyone has their own memories of starting school. I remember feeling very fortunate that my gran was able to give me money for tuck. I think it was 50c! Most of the other kids had to go home and eat. I hated that. Or they got leftover food from the night before, which I hated even more. I wanted *magwinya* – v*etkoek*, with polony and atchar. Once or twice, when gran didn't have money, I would also have to go home for lunch, but most of the time she spoiled me.

When my brother came back to stay with us, we became a family unit in Pimville again, and staying at Gran eventually became only a weekend thing.

Pimville was like the 'business end' of things – it was all about school and homework and chores; Mom was working; Dad was working. What I remember most were the TV shows! We would watch *The A-Team*, and *The Cosby Show*, and something called *Lapologa*. It was like a dance competition with these pantsula guys from all over the country. They would have like a dance-off. We just used to love it.

My dad used to hate it. He would always say things like he wished they knew their maths as well as they knew their dance moves.

My parents held that whole academic world in high regard. That's why my mom was always studying. But I believed, even though she wanted to further her education, she was really at her happiest when she was playing music. That's the other thing I remember from those years – there was a lot of music. My parents would have to vie with each other for turns on the record player, which was always interesting. They wouldn't exactly argue. My dad would try hog the record player, but my mother had her own tastes. She liked Dionne Warwick and Roberta Flack, Billy Ocean, Diana Ross and The Supremes. My dad was happiest when he played jazz. When I was growing up, I honestly thought that my dad played jazz music just to irritate me. With musicians like Brenda Fassie, Whitney Houston, the beat was simple; you could follow it. Jazz made no sense to me. I thought he did it to piss me off, and to annoy my mom. My dad had this massive collection of records – it was huge. My other gran, my dad's mom, she even used to say to my mom: 'If he buys one more record, you must go and buy another dress.' But of course my mom never did.

It took me a long time to appreciate the kind of music my dad played. When I was in my early twenties, while my dad was still alive, I remember us driving to a funeral. I knew we were going to be driving together, and so I had planned this whole thing, playing him Frank Sinatra in the car, trying to show off that I knew who Old Blue Eyes was. But my dad, in typical fashion, he didn't ask which album it was, or compliment my choice of music. He just said: 'Ugh! I've been playing Frank Sinatra for years, since before you were born.' He was acting like, what do you even know? Actually, I was very proud that he knew more about music than I did.

After my dad died I took almost his entire record collection and kept it in my house. What happened to it in the end was so sad. This one girl I had been seeing ... after we broke up, I confessed that I had cheated on her. So she took all those records and threw them away. I don't know where. I'd always had plans to create music from those records.

I guess I try speak up in my dad's defence, even though there was often this disconnect between us. He had three kids, all at private schools. It couldn't have been easy on the salary he earned. He was constantly having fights with my mom. My dad self-medicated with alcohol. When he was sober it was like there was this kind of cold war. When he was drunk, that was when he opened up and told us how much he loved us. But he had to get like that before he would show any kind of connection. I guess he was just trying to figure it out, like all of us.

Do we ever thank God for the mistakes our parents made? It's hard for me to say he made a mistake. That was just the way he was. Even if I could sit down with him now and try and talk about it, my dad had this way of ... not having an excuse really, but there was always a reason for things – he could always explain it – and that was that.

For my part, I also used to avoid talking about stuff with him because most of our interactions would expose my lack of progress in whatever area of my life was under discussion. I always had this feeling my dad was disappointed in me, that I did not turn into the guy he envisioned me to be. It was always strictly business with my dad, and maybe it was safer that way for both of us. He would mostly talk to me about my chores, or about school, or about visiting family. There was always something to do: have you polished the shoes; have you washed the takkies; go get the newspaper ... We could even be sitting and watching TV and my dad would try and turn it into some kind of lesson. When he was in the kitchen, cooking, he wouldn't show me how to make the food; he would just issue instructions: 'Bring me that tomato.' That was his way of teaching; he just wasn't able to engage in the way a kid needs his parent to engage with him. Sometimes he would be sitting listening to music, or watching TV, and he would call me from my bedroom. 'Kabelo, get me some juice,' he would say. And then I would bring him his juice, and hang around for a few minutes, waiting, but he wouldn't say anything else, so I'd go back to my room. In hindsight, I realise that was his way of trying to reach out, but it failed.

It took a long time for me to realise how much I had learned from my dad. When I was older, when I had hit my head against the wall a couple of times, when TKZee started to become a success ... every single time, these lessons from my dad would start to come out: be honest. Don't lie. Always be three steps ahead of your competition. When he'd first said these things to me, I hadn't really listened. My dad wasn't particularly successful. I mean, we can ask what does 'success' mean anyway; but, money-wise, he wasn't this huge success. So I treated him like he didn't know anything. It was only when I got out into the world that all these things started to make sense, like I had just never heard them before.

When I started working in the music industry, that was the first time we really started to engage. Don't pay people to play your music, he would tell me. Don't pay *payola* (paying other people money to get your songs played). When I got nervous about working with big names, he would remind me that all of the people I was intimidated by also had grandparents and mothers and fathers. When he said that it just made everybody normal; it actually helped a lot. Even then, he was often still very critical. When I was 22 years old I bought myself a new BMW M3. He said to me: 'You better watch this car. It's not just about buying it and paying it off. You've got to do maintenance, you've got to pay for petrol, you've got to look after the tyres.' When I started making proper money, I used to give money to my brother and my sister. What I thought of as extra pocket money. When my dad found out, he completely freaked out at me. He said it was better if I gave him the money, that they needed to learn how to fend for themselves. He told me I was crippling them.

If he was alive today, I think we would have made up the time, because I finally get it. In rehab, they tell you: don't try and change your parents, don't try change your father. If anyone has to change in this relationship, it is you.

It's a bit different with my mother. If one acknowledges that, in a perfect world, the mistakes of the past propel one to a better life in the future, she would probably say, please learn from my mistakes.

As a kid, I was always aware that my mom was ambitious. I feel like maybe life just got in the way of that – life, kids, challenges. My mom dreamed much bigger. Her friends were always studying; she was always telling us this person got that degree ... but the pressures in her own life meant she didn't follow through for herself. I don't know if this made her resentful, especially when we hit financially hard times, or when my dad was drinking. But I always wished it for her, that she could have carried on with her dreams.

I was never a mommy's boy, or a granny's boy. That tag team of my mom and my gran, it worked because they had such a great relationship; it was never like my mom just dropped me off and left. The one was like an extension of the other. But I knew I was a kid who was loved, and that always made me feel, subconsciously, like everything was going to be okay.

When it comes to family, the good stuff is easy. But for me it is really about sticking together – I can see that in my mom's relationship with my dad. Family is like a net. It's a place where you can fall back, with your back to that net, and know that you will be caught.

When I acknowledge my parents' mistakes in the context of me being fully aware of them just being human, wanting to give their best, I can understand that no parent can ever get it 100% right. That blesses a parent's heart: you did this, and maybe that wasn't so cool, but you know what – thank you so much for everything, because I've lived life now and I have understood that one can be faced with myriad challenges. Even through all of that, you still persevered, and I am who I am because of you.

The Hills in Your Mind

On an up run, you start climbing about 10 kilometres into the race – there are a few steep gradients before then, but, just after Westville, the route dips, and then you have to work your way up the first of what they call the 'Big Five' hills: Cowies Hill.

By the time you're over it, you're about 20 kilometres into the race and your body is warm. But, in your mind, you know there are *five* big hills and you've just done the one. At this point it's all about preservation. It's about finding the balance between preserving your energy, and still delivering a good enough pace to hit your timing splits. It's a very uncomfortable place to be. The watch is your enemy. Sometimes you're ahead of your split, but you know that means you're not saving enough energy to keep up the same pace for the rest of the race. If you expend your energy too fast, you know that it's going to catch up with you later on.

You Must Always Fight Back

When I was about six or seven years old, there was this kid in Pimville who started bullying me. Whenever I went to play with the other kids in the street, he would always be on my case. It was like having a thorn stuck in my flesh – nothing big, just that he never, ever let up. He was taller than me, but I think we were about the same age. My anger had been building for quite a while, but one afternoon I decided I was sick and tired of taking it, and I finally stood up to him. I can remember exactly where it was – on the street, just next to that patch of green grass outside our house. I started screaming, at him; I lashed out with my fists. After that day he stopped. I think later we may have even become friends. That moment is so significant for me growing up. I felt liberated; it made me feel different about myself. Later in life, the pushing, the taunting – it was a constant, particularly when I went to boarding school. If you didn't stand up for yourself there, you would be taken out. I felt sorry for the guys who didn't have it in them to stand up for themselves and fight back.

I think my mom and dad tried to shelter me from how they grew up. They lived in the heart of this country's worst era. They never had the opportunity to get a good education. My mom talks about when black students wanted to apply to study at Wits University, They had to get permission from the Minister of Education. There were black universities for them, and they were not easily accepted at white universities. That was their point of reference for raising us: whatever they had been denied, their kids wouldn't have to experience the same hardships.

When I started Grade 2 I was enrolled at a private primary school in Mayfair, called Mayfair Convent. Every morning I would have to wake up at 5 am, and I would get picked up between 6 am and 6.30 am in a kombi – I used to call it the 'kumbi' – by a guy who ran a transport service for other kids who also at the same school. He would fetch children from all over Soweto – from Meadowlands, Zola – and drive us to Mayfair. Because I was on the outskirts of Soweto I was always the last kid to get picked up, and the first to get dropped off at home.

On the kumbi, everybody spoke different languages – they came from different locations. It was like this constant exchange. And then we would get to Mayfair and ... it wasn't like you had to put your Soweto-ness behind you, but you had to walk in to school and you had to deal with Sister Ursula the headmistress, and you had to deal with it on their terms, play the game using their rules. And you *had* to play the game. So you would do your flute practice and choir and chapel. And then, later on, at 2 pm or 3 pm, the kumbi came again and picked you up, and you went back to Soweto.

This was right in the middle of a very volatile political time in Soweto, but as kids we were mostly oblivious to it. You were just going to school while the country was burning. I remember when I was in about Standard 2 (Grade 4), it was the middle of the State of Emergency. For a while we couldn't go to school at all. We were kept at home and, obviously, if you're a kid and you're at home and there's no school, you're going to run around the neighbourhood with your friends. We wound up running away from cops instead. I remember watching a Casspir shooting tear gas into houses, and then we just ran and hid under a broken-down truck that was on the side of the road. We were lying there, watching the Casspir from under the truck and hoping it wouldn't turn towards us. All we could see was the Casspir's wheels. I remember being particularly scared because I was also where I was not supposed to be, quite far away from home, and I knew that if my mother found out, then I would be in even more trouble!

From the time I arrived at Mayfair Convent, I can remember almost everything. It was amazing. There was a white teacher; there were black kids and coloured kids and Indian kids. And I was like: what kind of place *is* this?

I remember the teacher trying to speak to me in English – her name was Mrs Judith Lacey, and she was a godsend. Her husband and my dad both worked together at Liberty Life. The first day I arrived, she tried to ask me something. I can't remember exactly what she said, because I couldn't speak any English. I still don't know what kind of sentence I put together when I tried to reply. But that day is the last day I remember not being able to speak English. After that it was all 'Ben the Dog' and 'Felix the Cat', and Judith Lacey, who was sweet and caring and nurturing. I took to that environment like a fish to water.

The school houses at Mayfair Convent were red, yellow and blue. I was in the blue house, Marian; red was Mercy, and yellow was Lourdes. We used to do sprints, and I remember being really good at them. I can't remember if I won any races, but I'd like to believe that I did. The school grounds were set up so that, during break, pretty much all the activity was concentrated on the two netball courts and a single tennis court. The girls all went to play netball, and the cool guys went to the tennis court. So, in Standard 1 (Grade 3), I started playing tennis, and I ended up being really good at it. By the time I reached Standard 5 (Grade 7), I was number two in the whole school. The number one player was my friend Grant Sauls.

Tennis was the first thing I was really committed to. I was a bit obsessed even. I tried a few other extramurals at school, like recorder – which was boring – and even first aid. I qualified and got a certificate, and then I found out you had to keep renewing it every year and I thought stuff that, and didn't do it again.

During break time we were always on the tennis court, trying to beat the older guys. This carried over when I was at home in Soweto. I watched tennis on the TV and I knew all the players. I would go and practise at local schools – I practised a lot! – hitting balls against a wall over and over and over again. Sometimes my neighbourhood friends would come and join in and try play, but they couldn't really play for anything. My uncle played tennis at varsity, which kind of made it acceptable within my family, but my parents never really got it, and they couldn't afford to buy me the kit that I wanted. It didn't register with them. My dad said I was just trying to be like all the other kids at school.

Tennis and music. Those were the two things I really wanted from my parents: great tennis gear, and a boom box. The only racket my parents ever bought me was when I was in Standard 5. I *really* wanted a graphite racket; my mom bought me an aluminium one. I think I used it once or twice, just to show that I had, but I didn't like it. Grant always used to hand me down his shoes, his rackets, his racket bags. He came from a well-off family, and always had the latest Wilson or Dunlop, and he would just pass his old ones on to me. So there I was, wearing his tennis shoes, playing with his tennis rackets. It was only towards the end of primary school that it occurred to me maybe I was leeching off him a little bit.

I also remember thinking that the other kids' lunches always looked better than mine. I used to hate lunch from home. Half the time I just wouldn't eat it. I'd throw my food under the bed, then, two or three weeks later I would find these mouldy sandwiches lying there. It was the worst when my dad would make my lunch – he would only make cheese and tomato sandwiches, which were completely boring and uninteresting. You could actually tell when food had been made by my dad, just by tasting it. My mom cooked most of the time, but sometimes my dad would come home and say, 'I'm cooking.' And you knew, immediately, that food had been cooked by a man. It was just hard. Even when he made pap.

My dad used to try teach me financial fitness by giving me R20 for the tuckshop at school, and telling me I was supposed to make it last for a week or two. I'd blow it in like three days – I would buy sodas, chocolates, nigger balls. I'd actually go ask for them by that name. There's Kabelo going, 'Can I have a nigger ball?' Even the teachers would say it. I mean, what were they thinking? I guess none of us ever really thought about it, about what we were actually saying.

The black and white thing really only started to become a feature for me once I had finished at Mayfair Convent and started high school. I spent my first year at Sacred Heart College in Observatory. Pretty much everyone from Mayfair was going to Sacred Heart, and initially it was where I thought I wanted to go too – but when I got there I felt like there was something missing. It was really hard, starting fresh. It was a much bigger school and a lot of the kids there had come up from the Sacred Heart primary school so they already knew each other. Even with the people I knew from Mayfair I still felt like an outsider, and that mattered to me.

I tried to carry on with tennis, but suddenly I was in a school with a lot more competition, and Grant had gone to a different high school so he wasn't there to give me his gear any more. At Sacred Heart they played soccer – although I watch it and love it now, I wasn't necessarily very excited about soccer then, except when we used to play during break times, which was more social soccer, not on a field – and they swam. I didn't swim. I still can't swim.

Girls were also a problem. I had fallen 'in love' with this one girl. She was a year younger – she must have been in Standard 5. I don't know exactly how we decided this, but suddenly we were going out, and I was all excited because I had never kissed a girl before. Obviously I was very eager to do so. I sent her a letter. I don't know exactly what I wrote, the usual stuff: I dig you. Big Time. And then I added that I thought it was time for us to 'graunch'. That was the word flying around those days – you didn't kiss someone, you 'graunched' them.

She told everybody.

I was the laughing stock of the school. Then we broke up. And I didn't get to kiss her after all. Everything after that was just long and hard. Sacred Heart wasn't a really pleasant experience for me. Academically I was surviving, but, for the first time, I was up against really brilliant students. Everything about the school was just much bigger. It would be a stretch to say that I hated it. More than anything, I think I was intimidated by change.

I never said anything to my mom, but somehow she saw how unhappy I was – she calls it my 'erratic behaviour'. At the end of the year she told me that I wasn't going back.

Because my mom was a teacher, she was obviously privy to educational opportunities. Every weekend she would take me out of Diepkloof, and make me attend extramurals and extra classes as part of a gifted child programme that helped kids from Soweto. The programme also reached out to private schools like St John's and St Stithians, and one weekend I went to go and write the entrance exam for St Stithians ('Saints'). I passed, and the next year I was enrolled – repeating Standard 6 (Grade 8). The outreach programme was going to pay for everything; all we had to pay for was my uniform, and my books.

Saints for me felt the same as I had felt on my first day at Mayfair Convent. Everything in the place was amazing. Before the term started, one of the parents organised a meet-and-greet braai, at Richard Parry's in Bryanston. That's where I met Warren Hickinbotham, who was like my Grant Sauls of St Stithians, and who is still my friend today. Warren's family basically took me in – they were my family outside of my family.

I felt like I'd been given a fresh start. I'd never been to an all-boys' school, and there was a moment of intense relief when I thought: boys' school, no distraction from females, no pressure. At Sacred Heart the pressure was all about who was dating who, and I had found myself really challenged in that department. That was a big part of being in a co-ed school: Valentine's Day, school socials ... a lot of your value was based on how well you interacted with the opposite sex, and I was failing badly. In primary school it had been a lot safer; a crush was a non-starter.

Saints was steeped in tradition, and I completely took to it. I loved being a skivvy, the hierarchy between the boys, the ranks and privileges. You had to earn your stripes, your colours, for academics, sport ... There was order and respect. There was a food chain. It was the first time I had been to a school that had a school song. When I did my prefect's exam, I had to learn the history of the school. I still think that's flipping awesome.

I became a boarder. I fell in love with rugby; I was in absolute heaven. It was the best thing my mom could have done for me – thank God she had the presence of mind to move me from Sacred Heart, and to let me repeat the year. I don't know what I would have done if I'd matriculated in 1994. I wound up spending most of my weekends at the school, too, during term time. More because I wanted to be at Saints than not wanting to be at home.

There were two things that really worked in my favour at Saints: first, the lack of pressure in having no girls; second, the company of other boys. Saints was where I first met Tokollo Tshabalala. We were in the same dormitory together. Standard 6s were all put into the big dormitory; as you got older, the dorms would get smaller and smaller. Before I met Tokollo, I'd only really seen the white side of St Stithians. This was the first time I'd met another black kid. He was there in the dorm room with his earrings and his chains. Always anti-establishment, from day one. And nothing's really changed!

David Mdaka was also there – he had actually been at Progress High School in Soweto, where my mom taught, which I thought was a weird coincidence. My skivvy master was a guy called Lebo Mosaka. He was like a hero to me: a black guy who was a prefect, head of house, who played first team water polo. It made me cool, being Lebo's skivvy – actually, he got to have two skivvies because he was head of house – but I used to polish his shoes, make his bed, tidy his room, make him coffee in the morning and make him hot chocolate when he was studying. I would go pick up his laundry.

And I just had this confidence that I could be away from home. I was ready to be a 'big boy'; I was kind of big anyway, in addition to being pretty full of myself. I don't know if it was from growing up in Soweto, that gave me something of an edge. Saints could be like the Wild West. I know it's a stereotype of boarding schools, but you had to lay down the law right from the beginning, otherwise it was tickets for you. Tokollo also had this bravado; there was a sense that he was larger than life.

At Saints, what tended to happen was that the black kids grouped together. But I would always break that mould, because that wasn't how I saw my life. I was very fortunate in that integration had been the norm for me from a very early age. I'm so grateful for those formative years ... what happens then will be normal for the rest of your life.

All in all, there were probably 15, maybe 20 black guys in the whole school, out of 600 boys. Having gone to Mayfair and Sacred Heart had already exposed me to a lot of different cultures. I'd gone to school with affluent white kids before, so it wasn't anything new or difficult or strange for me. It was easy for me, in a way, not to be 'aware' of my blackness in a setting like St Stithians. The circumstances of my childhood had allowed me to understand the person who had Ramadan and Eid, just as easily as a white Christian boy from the suburbs.

What was funny was that at boarding school I would hang out with Tokollo and David, but at school we were in different classes and so I would spend my time with Warren, with all the white kids.

There was always this kind of tension. Not *always* always. But it was there. There are always guys wanting to prove they are more black than you. The black guys started calling me Jungle Fever. Tokollo and David actually still call me Jungle. At one point we stopped talking. For months. It was like a stupid boys' stand-off. Then, one night, I was listening to music in the dormitory. I used to sleep with earphones in every night. They probably weren't even my earphones – I probably borrowed them, and I probably borrowed someone else's music tape too. Tokollo complained that he could hear the music coming out my earphones, and he just jumped out of bed and pulled them off my head. And then he started listening to what I was listening to, and he thought it was cool. And that just broke the tension. From then on, we were best of friends again.

One of the things I learned – not just from boarding school, but also from working in the music industry – is that part of standing up for yourself, part of being able to express yourself and make yourself heard, is about whether or not the environment you are in is safe for you. And if it's not, then you have to create that safe space for yourself, mentally. You will only really express your *self* in a safe environment, and if you don't learn how to speak up or speak out, or share your opinion, you are always going to feel stifled.

When you're in a recording studio ideas are a dime a dozen. Some are great, some are crap. And you have to share your ideas, even when you're afraid they might be wrong or that others won't like them. Your ego, your self-esteem might hold you back, might make you self-conscious. Or you might tell yourself: I'll only share my thoughts when this particular other person is around. But they won't be there all the time. You will. And if your voice or your opinions remain only with you, they won't benefit anyone else.

Letting Go of a Situation Doesn't Mean Letting Go of Who You Are

> *As a teenager, music, for me, was mostly about being a consumer, not a musician or a performer. I was in the school choir, and – once – I entered this talent search. I remember going to Bryanston High School, rapping and beat-boxing in front of everyone in the school hall. I didn't win. I tried acting in a few school plays. Zwai Bala directed one of them. He got to play the intellectual. We were the rabble-rousers. I was the head of the mob. We had to break stuff and toyi-toyi.*

At Saints my tennis obsession became a thing of the past. There the standard was *proper* high. I think there were eight tennis teams, and I was playing in the fourth. The guys who were on the first team were basically at the level of professional players. For some reason I thought I would take up hockey instead – it had a stick, and a ball, and I suppose I thought maybe it would be a good compromise between tennis and soccer. I never even got to play. One of the rugby coaches saw me faffing around at a hockey practice. 'Hey, Mabalane,' he said. 'You're too big for hockey. Come try rugby.'

Before then, I had never played rugby a day in my life. I'd always thought of it as an Afrikaans sport. My first year wasn't great at all. I was in the front row, playing prop, and I remember absolutely *hating* it. I was unfit, and I was overweight. They used to call me Heavy K and they called Tokollo 'Heavy T', because we were both fat. Or maybe we were chunky. Running around when you are chunky and unfit is *really* unpleasant.

But I fell in love with rugby gradually as I started to understand the sport. The game-changer for me was the day I got to see the Saints first XV play. They had a different uniform to the rest of the school, and when they played, it was compulsory for the whole school to watch. The first team match was the last game of the day. When the under-13s played, it was early in the morning and there was still dew and ice on the grass, and hardly anyone came to see us. By the time the first team came on, it was afternoon and everyone was at the game; the ground was packed. That was the incentive: I wanted to be those guys. They were the heroes. You would watch the guy playing your position, and want to be him. Everyone at the school wore blue scarves, but the first team guys, they wore white scarves. That was the start of the dream.

With tennis, I had always equated playing well with having the best equipment: graphite rackets, new shoes ... rugby stuff was easy, I could get jerseys and socks at the swap shop. And, besides, rugby was like *the* school sport. Come winter time, St Stithians was a rugby school.

As I started understanding the game, my skills also got honed. It's what happens when you're a boarder: touch rugby is basically your favourite pastime. So you're constantly running, training, eating to keep up your energy. Over time your skill gets better. It makes sense that it would, if you were doing something regularly.

There was a notice board at school where they would post the names of the guys who had made the sports teams. I started off in the

C team and made my way up to playing in the B team – the B team always trained with the A team; the C team trained with the D team – but the A team always eluded me. I made the under-13 B, the under-14 B ... By Standard 8 (Grade 10) I guess I had started showing some kind of potential. I was asked to train with the under-15s, and we all went to Durban as part of a tournament team. I must have been the youngest player on the bus; I even remember that I had a number 16 sweater. I wasn't on the side that got to play, but I was named as part of the squad; and when that happened, my confidence really started to come up.

By that stage I was already starting to get quite competitive. I finally started to play a few games on the under-15 A team. At that stage, you could choose whether you wanted to play under-15s or opens. I remember going to open trials, and I made the third team but quickly got dropped down to the fifth team. By Standard 9 (Grade 11) I was back to playing the third team again. At that stage, you must understand, it was make or break for me. Matric was the following year, and playing rugby and making the first team was pretty much all I was thinking about. I was doing training off-season; I was doing rowing in summer. I was completely committed to it.

When matric rolled around, we got through the summer months, through January, February. Then came the big trials. The first team got named.

And I didn't make it.

But I did get named as the captain of the second team. So I thought, at least I'm captain. And the second team also got to play in different uniforms. I played my heart out in that team. I kept trying to make the first team – and eventually I did. I remember calling my mom to tell her. We had to make a pilgrimage to McCullagh & Bothwell, the school uniform shop in Hyde Park. I remember saying to the shop assistant: 'We'd like the St Stithians first team jersey please.' It was white, with the school badge; the rugby socks were blue and white.

I had made the first team because I'd been chosen for the annual rugby festival squad. And, in my first game for the first team, at St Stithians rugby festival, I got injured. I was literally only on the field for 10 or 15 minutes. How's that for a flipping sad story?

After that, it was school holidays, and when term started again I went back to being the second team captain. I played my heart out, again; and, again, I made the first team. There was that white jersey. Those jerseys were like everything to us. Actually, the one match we wore red. The red jersey! We only wore it if one of the visiting teams that was playing also had a white jersey. The last time I'd seen the red jersey was when I was in Standard 6. It made a really big impression on me. I got to wear the red jersey. Flip, that was amazing. I get excited thinking about it all over again.

The entire way through my matric year I was in and out of the first team. But to be honest, I always had more fun when I played in the second team. We were the school's best second team in like a long time; we would beat these Afrikaans high schools that hadn't been beaten in a long time. All of us were in and out of the first team. But we had more fun when we played seconds because there was so much less pressure. I would often get carried away in my role as captain. After every practice I would make everyone line up on the touchline and do push-ups until *I* said we were done. And those boys would actually listen. They were my peers. After practice, they would treat me like a normal dude. But on the pitch, they respected me. We had been taught to respect that hierarchy.

Even my social life was anchored around rugby. Standard 9, I got put into the same class as all the guys I would later captain, and we glorified our incapabilities – we laughed at ourselves. We were the thick class. By the time we got to matric, we actually celebrated it: 10B, the doff class. But that label also left me with a point to prove; I always knew there was something better, waiting. I think the other guys in my class must have felt the same way because the 10B guys I bump into now turned out to be awesome individuals. We didn't just accept that we were doff, and then roll over and die.

Up until Standard 8, my schoolwork, academics, had been good – I was flying even. Then it changed. Midway through Standard 8 the maths got more difficult. The French, the biology, *everything* got more difficult. My learning and my studying should have grown proportionally, but it faltered; I faltered. The best place I could be was on the rugby field. Or in English class. We had the most fantastic teacher, Miss Jill Worth. That woman is one of the people who changed my life.

Miss Worth was very arty. She was how I imagined a proper English teacher should be. In the classroom there were Athol Fugard posters, and probably a U2 poster. When we had triple English, I was in heaven.

One day, when it was getting close to exams, Miss Worth told the class something really important. She said that, in life, there were many different kinds of smart. There was life smart, there was academic smart, there was street smart, music smart ... That was quite a revelation for me – that I didn't necessarily have to be academically smart. She reignited some hope in me, that whichever way the cookie crumbled I would be fine. She also said that real men buy flowers for their own homes. That comment and the 'smart' thing really stuck with me.

I think that I was a really curious teenager; I had an inquisitive nature. But I held myself back from asking questions, or from asking the right questions. Now, when there's something that I don't know, I go and find out about it. I look at my music career – I'd never made a piece of music before TKZee. Zwai was the one who knew how to do things, and he was the one who would feed me information. I was always asking him questions. The other day I sent him a text message, saying that it was because of him I'd learned all this stuff. He wrote back saying he was proud of me, and that I had always been willing to learn! Maybe it was the subject matter that made it easier, but it also has a lot to do with the teacher. By the time I got to Bible College, I had learned a lot about ... learning I suppose. I learned that if you actually *listen* in class, everything starts falling into place. That was when I realised that I *could* do this. I do have it in me. But, back then, in high school, I didn't know that I did.

The year I finished school was the year that South Africa won the Rugby World Cup. It was 1995. I'd played first team rugby for St Stithians. A rugby career seemed like a viable option for me. It seemed entirely possible that I could become a Springbok rugby player, and I guess the fact that there weren't any black players on the side only served to inspire me. I saw myself like I was at school – I would be the black guy, in the midst of all these white guys.

At home it was a different story. My parents were against sports from day one. My dad would tell me I was messing around. 'You think you those bloody white kids. You're not those white kids,' he would say. My mom was also disappointed I think. But, one day, she said to me: you can be whatever you want to be.

I've mentioned that when I was at Saints I didn't often go home on weekends during term time. Maybe it was about avoiding difficult conversations with my parents about my life; or me not wanting to see them having arguments about their own lives – but that was only a small part. I also didn't want to bother my mom, make her drive out after work to fetch me, then have to bring me all the way back on Sunday. And there was a group of boarders at school who were from Soweto. We would decide, together, if we were all going to stay for the weekend. Then we'd get videos and hang out together. On other weekends I would go home with Warren and stay with his family. I usually only went home when term was up.

When you straddle both worlds, you're constantly having to prove that you are who you are – at Saints, at boarding school, maybe even more so back home in Soweto. But when I look back at my upbringing, and at my experiences, I've always believed there has been real purpose to it – not just because it shaped me, and allowed me to be who I am, but also because I think there are other people who will benefit from what I learned and the way I grew up. Maybe my purpose is to be almost like a ... leader, in the times we now find ourselves in. I've been exposed to so many parts of this country. I feel like I can play a role in helping to reconcile these different parts. Even when I was at Saints, I was aware of this. There were some kids who would arrive, fresh from Soweto and they weren't necessarily scared, but they might have been intimidated by the surroundings – and I was able to be a bridge for them because I understood both worlds, and I understood them well. When you understand what both worlds are like, when you actually speak both languages, you are able to relate to people a lot more easily. You can decode things that otherwise get lost in translation.

Part of this was also 'demystifying' the black person to the white person, and vice versa. I had to be the voice that spoke out, when my white friends in their white world would say things without thinking, without really understanding what they had said. I'd often get told things like: 'Kabs, you're not like those other blacks. You're not like those blacks at the taxi ranks.' I guess they thought it was some kind of compliment? I'd literally have to point it out to them, why what they were saying wasn't just wrong, it was really unacceptable. But I didn't get offended, there were no heated arguments. These were my friends, and I knew that, when I was correcting them, they were speaking from an ignorant point of view. They would listen to me. It's also difficult for me to say, categorically, that white people are bad. Some white people have played really significant roles in my life. And being invited into the suburbs, spending time there, allowed me to dream. It allowed me to dream of being more. I knew what the other side of the tracks looked like, and it wasn't always pretty. I felt like I had been given permission by my mom to dream whatever I wanted to be, and that allowed me to make my world, and my dreams, much bigger. Why shouldn't I want the same things, similar things, as my white counterparts? It didn't make me any less a boy from Soweto.

And I loved it in Soweto. I had proper friends there. I never felt like a foreigner, but I always felt special. I would go away for three or four months at a time, then I'd come back and tell all my friends war stories about boarding school and rugby, and being at school with Chinese kids and German kids.

We had our own fun. It was all about the music – who had the latest album – and about shoes, about sneakers, about the girl that you liked, and hopefully managed to get it right with in the holidays. I would spend the whole holiday making plans to go and speak to just one girl. And then I would actually see her, and get scared and run away.

A lot of my friends were also at private schools, so I didn't stick out like a sore thumb. My mom's generation – all their children ... they made sure they got a great education. They wanted a better life for all of us. As much as people want to glorify living in Soweto, people want better lives for their children.

When we left Pimville (in 1986 or 1987), we stayed with my gran for a bit while our house in Diepkloof was being built, and then we moved into this new, bigger house in Phase 3. There it was like the suburbs. That was where I met my friend Thuli Tillis. His family had also moved to Diepkloof. His mom and my mom became best friends; our families knew each other – we became like family in a way.

Thuli had originally come from Ghost Town, and he knew the more dangerous parts of Soweto, the places and the people I suppose I had been protected from. From the time we were teenagers, Thuli and I would go to Ghost Town, go to Zola together, and he would tell me things, teach me things. Thuli was my window into another kind of life, and I was his window in turn – he also wanted better things for himself. It was a super-cultural exchange. We were young when our parents, their generation, had been involved in the struggle. Thuli's uncles were like comrades – they were the ones who were asking how we were going to fight. My uncles, they were the guys who were thinking how to overturn the system. We came from parallel but different places.

Thuli would often tell me gangster stories; he'd show me some of the gangsters. Sometimes we used to go wash the gangsters' cars to make money. Like I said, everyone wants a better life – especially when you have come from the gutter. Where do you think the gangsters moved to when they made money? They came to Diepkloof Extension. And they had these fast, flashy cars, their VR6 Golfs,

BMW 325is, the ones we called *gusheshe*, or the *isandla semfene*, the 535i. These guys would rob banks, or steal, or do whatever, and then they would come and park at the local spaza shop. The lighties walking around on the street, that was us – and so we were the ones who washed their cars. It was always so close, that life. You would always hear stories about how successful someone had become, cash heists, robberies, spoils. The opposite also happened. You'd be in the 'hood and hear so-and-so got arrested, someone got shot. There were deaths. But I had so much momentum in my life; I had too many positive influences. Sports was huge for me.

I remember, once, going to rugby practice with a friend of mine, Lesego Legoete – we used to call him 'Chief'. Lesego had gone to Mondeor High, and he was a great rugby player. This was after we had finished school; we must have been heading to a practice at varsity. There we were, off to play rugby, and these two other friends of ours asked for a lift. They were the same age as us; they had grown up with us. But they had decided: stuff that, we're going to rob and steal. For them it was all about fashion, and cars, and money I suppose. They had given themselves over. And they got into the back of the van in Diepkloof, and, as we got to Nasrec, they said that was where they wanted to get out and do their business; they both had guns with them. You see, to us that was normal. They were off to rob and steal, and we were off to rugby practice.

A few years later I went to the one guy's funeral. He had been shot and killed during a house robbery. The other guy, I don't know where he is. Lesego, of course, is now a professional rugby referee. He's an amazing talent.

That was life: you come back from Saints, you come home for your holidays. These guys are your friends; they're not outsiders, people you don't know. They live in your neighbourhood. They also have dreams and aspirations. How they go about getting them is questionable, but you feel for them. When you're a teenager you even admire them on a certain level – they're doing that whole gangster-life thing. And, truth be told, there was always the temptation. It was always there.

When I was in about Standard 8, someone I knew had a gun. They showed it to me, and then they gave it to me to take home. I kept the gun in a backpack under my bed, and I had it for a really long time – for quite a few months. Eventually the person who had given it to me asked for it, and I gave it back and I moved on. But you don't know. When you have a gun in your hands you don't know what you're going to do with it. I know what it felt like when I had a tennis racket in my hand; everything just felt right. It clicked. Imagine if this clicked, having a gun in my hand? When my sports career faltered and I started spending a lot more time doing drugs, drinking ... I look at that and I have to thank God for my music taking off when it did, otherwise who knows what would have happened if it didn't. Of course, the music enabled my addiction, which would turn into a whole other story.

You know, maybe I was lucky when I was younger; maybe I was able to navigate those worlds – Saints, Soweto, my parents, my friends, gangsters, rugby players – because I was always very sure of who I was. Going to Saints didn't make me any more *or* less black.

Authenticity has always been very important to me – I think this has a lot to do with my dad, and how he drummed the importance of honesty and hard work into me. When my music career started to take off, that became even more significant: how could I make my music ring true?

Thuli was a big part of keeping me connected to that – we were best friends; we were always together in Diepkloof. When I would go back to Soweto, we would hang out and chill at this spot, Magesta. Those gangsters, those were the guys I would play my music to once I had finished recording in the studio. Later on, Thuli started getting into the music business. We wrote songs together. Quite a few of my biggest hits were ones I had co-written with him. He performed with me as well, and he also became really good friends with Tokollo. After Thuli died, that was when I really experienced a big disconnect. After that I didn't go to the 'hood as much.

I had already been clean for a year when Thuli was killed. We'd been in studio, working on stuff for my new album. I'd been trying to talk to him about changing his life, cleaning up. When we finished for the night I took him home. I thought that whatever we had been talking about had started to sink in, because that evening he actually said to me: 'I'm not going out tonight. Drop me off at home.' But then another friend of his came and picked him up, later, and they went out drinking. They had a car accident on the way home. The driver survived, but Thuli was killed.

I was never a gangster, but I grew up with gangsters. And I was a drunk, and I was an addict. Now I realise I have to be ... not *that guy*. I have to be the evolution of that guy. I think this is very important. That is a very important role. It *was* about drugs, and sex, and rock and roll, and about being tough. My life was about that, and my music was about that. But I've cleaned up.

I'm still making music for the same people – although now maybe my scope is broader, I'm still producing music for people in the 'hood. That music comes from there, that's who I am through and through, and I'll never forget where I came from – or the people who supported me, the people who bought my music, the person I married. My wife is also from there, although she comes from the 'Soweto' of Kimberley.

This life never leaves you, even if you leave the life.

Make the 'Big Picture' Simple

I'm an introvert on the road. I pull my cap down low and stick in my earphones, and generally try avoid making contact with other runners. I don't want to talk to anybody until we hit maybe the last 10 kilometres of a race. I really believe energy expenditure even comes down to words, and I want to put all my energy into my run. I feel bad sometimes, because guys will want to chat. But, when I'm in a race, it's not the time or place.

Over-thinking is also a drain on your energy. When your mind is ticking, constantly trying to calculate never-ending numbers – the pace on every kilometre, every small milestone – you just wear yourself down. Breaking a race like Comrades into hundreds of minute components makes it overwhelming. If you split it into larger parts you can still evaluate your progress, still keep your eye on the bigger picture, but without getting bogged down in the detail. It's all about finding balance. Sometimes this means you need to step back. As soon as I start feeling a build-up of lactic acid in my legs, I make myself pause – I don't stop; in this race you must never stop moving forward – and I run for three lampposts, walk for one. I repeat this until my legs are ready to move again. You have to eat the elephant piece by piece.

I guess I have my own markers, not just the 'Big Five'. By the time I reach Hillcrest I know I've already run about 33 kilometres, and I still have a Two Oceans Ultra Marathon to go (the Two Oceans route is 56 kilometres). On the down run, I'm congratulating myself for just finishing a Two Oceans – but I know there's still nearly three hours to go. Either way, it hurts.

The halfway mark comes at Drummond, in between Botha's Hill and Inchanga. If there is a milestone I pay attention to in Comrades, it's here. By the time I pass Botha's Hill I usually know whether I've got it right, or horribly wrong. If I'm on track at the halfway mark I know I'll be right for the next nearly 40-something kilometres too. In my first three races it was much easier for me to hit my halfway split. The faster I've got, the harder it's got. I'd love to get to a point where I hit halfway at *exactly* the right time, but I can never work it out perfectly. I come in too hot, or too slow. I'm still trying to work out how fast to come out, and how much to hold back.

The thing about the route is that before I run Comrades, the longest training run I have done, outside of races of course, is 28 kilometres. I know that training route off by heart; I know exactly where to hold back and where to give it horns. Comrades is so long that, even though I have run it eight times, I still haven't memorised it.

Music was My Last Resort

I fell in love with music listening to my parents play records. I would hear it, and I just got it. My brother and I used to sing songs together. Sometimes we would sing for my dad. One night, before we went to bed, he made us sing Whitney Houston's 'The Greatest Love of All' for him. I even had a special song book where I would write down all the song lyrics of my favourite tunes. When I was in primary school I once won a raffle, and the prize was an LP with a collection of the biggest hits of the year. It had that song 'Woodpeckers from Space', and tracks from Duran Duran and Bryan Ferry. It was proper 80s. I'm an 80s music freak. I think that's when all our best songs were written. By that time, I already had something like my own soundtrack. I can't articulate what it was. But the comfort thing that was there in my life? That was music.

The end of my matric year was the first time I had a drink. It was a little bit before exams. I was stressed out. I knew I was staring disappointment in the face. I never drank through school – I had always stayed away. My dad drank, and I loathed it because I saw what his drinking did to my family. Having an alcoholic as a father is ...

embarrassing. You're that kid who has *that* dad. You'll be playing with the other kids on your street, and you have to go through the awkwardness of your dad walking past you, pissed out of his skull. Once he'd walked past and was inside the house, it was all over, but, still, that moment could feel very long.

The same night I had my first drink – I think it was a cider – I also smoked marijuana. I was at a friend's house; who it was, exactly, I can't remember. There was a party, and I wound up smoking weed on the tennis court. I think we also ate some marijuana-laced banana bread.

St Stithians was the kind of school that really frowned on such behaviour. Because I was so involved in school sports, I didn't have time – or the guts to take a chance – before then. The end of matric just felt like it was the right time to experiment, and I had classmates with me who were also present at this naughty gathering, who had already been down that path. Their presence gave me a little bit of courage. There was this sense, for me, that I was no longer under authority, that I needed to lighten up a bit. The weird thing was that I didn't feel guilty at all. I just remember being excited about what the future held. I was running around, feeling carefree, and realising that I had stepped into a new world – and that it wasn't all that bad, because everything was going to be okay, and I felt safe. Even the most arbitrary thing was hilarious. My friends were happy, I was happy; what could possibly go wrong? There were girls at the party, too, which made that feeling, the optimism, even more vivid. I had a serious thing for one of the girls there, but I'd missed my opportunity earlier in the year. That night I was desperately trying to redeem myself. I didn't manage to 'land' her, but I can't recall that it dampened my mood.

I barely made it past matric. I was one of those kids who was regularly called into the office at school, and they always asked me, 'Son, what's going to become of your life?'

After pretty much *all* of my teachers had given me a talking to, one of them, a guy called Mr McCallum took me aside and asked if I was interested in taking part in a short-term student exchange – if I wanted to go and see the world. I had just decided to turn down a first XV rugby tour to England, which I had been looking forward to the whole year, so Mr McCallum's intervention was kind of like a godsend. And he really didn't have to help me – I had given him so much uphill at school; he had taught me history.

It was arranged that I would spend three months in Florida, in the United States. Which also meant that I would be very, very far away from home when I got my matric results, and hopefully my parents would be too busy missing me and worrying about me to be angry.

The Rotary programme was partially subsidised, but my dad had to come up with the rest of the cash. To this day, I don't know how he managed it – and, to be honest, at the time I didn't care. I treated it as if it was my right. At the airport I remember my dad just crying. He had never been overseas, never been on a plane. He had worked so hard just so that I could do those things. And I was still arrogant. It was my first time on a plane, but you could have sworn it was my hundredth time, the way I acted. Like it was nothing. It's just the way I was.

We were there at the airport with all these other students, from all over South Africa. The first flight was to Zurich, after which we were all catching connecting flights to wherever we were going. I was in transit at Zurich, and I sneaked out of the airport – it was flipping cold! – and then went straight back in, just so I could say, 'I've been to Zurich.'

From there I flew on to Dallas, and then to Florida, where I went to stay with a nice family in Boca Raton. I must say that when I got there it was a bit of an anti-climax. My vision of the States was DJ Jazzy Jeff, and this was suburbia. It was quiet. I moved into my room, spent my days mostly lazing around the house. One of the dad's friends took me to Hooters. I watched lots and lots of TV. I went to one or two schools, and gave talks about where I was from. I think a lot of that trip only really made sense to me when I got back to South Africa. Because it was only when I got home that I realised I had literally been halfway around the world. It made me realise that the possibilities were endless.

I remember going to a party that these kids literally had in their garage – it was in the middle of that garage-band explosion, and there was a band, a singer, a drummer, and the band was playing their own songs. It was really different to South Africa, where we would have had a DJ.

I spent time between Boca Raton and Miami, and then went to stay in Orlando with an ex-South African family. They were lovely, but it was also very suburban. I became obsessed with finding the ghetto. I'd tried to do it when I was in Boca, went to a place called Deerfield. I got a cab driver to take me through. It didn't look very pretty; I guess that's typical. I got there, and there were all these black guys on the sidewalk.

The family in Orlando had connections at NASA. They took me to Cape Canaveral, and I got given tours of all the space shuttles. The next thing I knew, we had a pass to go and watch a space shuttle launch in three days' time – I think it was going up to fix some satellite. We went to go see the actual shuttle that would be taking off, and I saw all the media cameras mounted around it; they would click on from the rocket's vibrations. On the day of the launch we woke up at about 2 am, when it was still dark dark. It was a quick drive from where they lived – it took us maybe 10 minutes to get to the viewing station at the other side of the river, on a lake of some sorts. There were people making eggs and bacon, the families and friends of the people who worked there. It was amazing. The clock, counting down, being able to see gallons of water gushing out from the shuttle, the sparks starting, and then it took off. The family I had stayed with in Boca could even see the lift-off, because it went so high! I was also invited to the landing, but I had to go back to South Africa.

I was dreading getting home. I thought I was going to have to do all my supplementary exams – that was my main focus: come home, sort out this matric thing, then go to university and play rugby at varsity. But the supps were really a schlepp. So I didn't do them. I wound up going to Wits Technikon and asking what course I could get into with the marks that I had, and that was how I started studying for a diploma in sports management.

In my mind, the actual degree was secondary to the rugby part. I had this idea that playing rugby at Wits Tech would somehow be my entry into a much bigger playing field. But school rugby turned out to be *very* different to varsity rugby. Those Afrikaans boys were *HUGE*, like they were all descended from Vikings or something. I practised with the under-21 B side, but at the games I just spent all my time on the bench. Eventually I thought, stuff this, I'm too small. And I left.

Music was my last resort. Turning music into a career happened, in a sense, because there was nothing else left that I *could* do.

Sometimes people's dreams don't happen because it's their own fault; sometimes it's just the fault of circumstances. I think I gave rugby an honest shot, but I wasn't good enough.

When you find yourself in that kind of situation, it's not necessarily time to give up. Don't buy property in the land of failure and disappointment. Dream another dream instead, and let creative persistence be your MO. You just have to keep moving.

Tokollo, Kabelo and Zwai, aka TKZee

TKZee started in a back room in a house in Linden. One of our favourite pastimes was to laugh together, at just about anything. We'd come up with the dumbest names for our act. One was 'Dangerous Darkies'. We'd say it, and then we would can ourselves. I remember one day, Zwai was on keyboard, and programming. Tokollo was sitting on a chair – really more like a short stool – and he had a cigarette in his hand and the mic in front of him, and he was just killing this rap verse. And in that moment we realised this dream was closer than we thought. That we could really have something to offer.

I'd actually been trying to push the music thing for quite a while. But I don't think my parents ever saw it as something that could be something.

When I was in Standard 8, Tokollo Tshabalala and I started a band. We called ourselves Two Slice. We were big Kris Kross fans in those days – we liked the attitude, the energy. Two guys feeding off each other's energy. There was another guy at school whose brother owned a studio, and it cost R400 for an hour. So we borrowed R400 from Tokollo's mom, and went to go and record a song. I think all we had at that stage were the lyrics. Our buddy's brother had to make the beat for us. There was no melody. We were just going to rap. That was our big plan.

Once we'd made the track we played it to a few people at school. We got ourselves a 'manager', a guy who was in matric, Tebogo Mokobo, and decided we were going to take our 'demo' to a music guy at EMI. We bunked school and took a taxi from Randburg all the way to the EMI offices in City Deep.

What I remember very specifically about that day was sitting and waiting. And waiting. And waiting. And waiting some more. Finally we were ushered into this huge office – typical record company style – and there was a guy in an armchair. For some reason there was a watermelon on the table. The next thing our tape – our cassette! – started blaring over the sound system, and everyone was listening to it and they were bobbing their heads. We thought we had made a really big impression.

We never got a call back.

I suppose the bigger the disappointment, the sweeter the victory. There were guys in that office, at that record company ... when our music started happening commercially, they were still struggling A&Rs ('Artist and Repertoires' – the guys in charge of finding new talent). They didn't even remember us from that time. But we remembered them.

Tokollo left St Stithians after 1993 and the music thing got poked – from a production point of view at least. I never stopped listening, or consuming. I collected so much music during that time. I would get music from other people, tapes, CDs; sometimes I'd be given music, and forget to return it. I guess I was known for that. I couldn't afford to buy my own, and I would get attached to tracks, to albums, to CDs.

Zwai Bala and I stayed on. Zwai was ahead of me and Tokollo at school; when he was in matric, I was his junior.

Zwai had been in the picture for a while, but at that stage he was doing much more serious musical stuff than Tokollo or I were doing. Zwai was in the school choir, and he sang with this other group called the Dukes, who were the top singers in the school. Sometimes he would play me gospel music, and classical music, but it wasn't the kind of music I listened to then. I didn't really get it, and, in a way, he didn't really get us either – but he could see that there was something there. We could all see something in each other.

After Zwai graduated he went to go study at the Royal Scottish Academy of Music and Drama in Glasgow. I finished matric the following year, and by that stage there wasn't any music happening in my life except for listening to it. I still think this is an important thing: for me, listening to music is just as good as reading books. Your music collection, your music library, it contributes to how you make music, it shapes what your influences are.

How the music thing got resurrected started with me barely passing matric, and going off to Florida on exchange. The day that I landed back in South Africa – literally, as we were driving back from the airport – I saw all these streetpole posters with Tokollo on them – he was in a band, he was on a poster! I rushed home and that afternoon another one of my friends gave me the Mashamplani CD. There was my guy, working with M'du Masilela and Sbu Ntshangase, and the late Pro Ngubane.

By the time I hooked up with Tokollo, Mashamplani was doing really well – they were exploding – but there was a lot of in-fighting, and the original line-up eventually broke up.

At around the same time, Zwai came back to South Africa. By

then he had made peace with sort of more street-influenced music. Somehow the three of us all ended up together again, in Linden, in the back room of the house where Zwai used to stay. And that was the start of TKZee.

Zwai wasn't from Johannesburg – he was from Port Elizabeth – but he stayed with a family in Joburg, and they had a back room that they let us turn into a makeshift studio. It was almost like an old storeroom, but it was a place we could work. There was a desk, and a couch. Sometimes we'd take the cushions off the couch to make an extra mattress on the floor when we needed to sleep. We wound up working and sleeping there, the three of us.

Musically, Zwai was the one who knew what was going on. He could play anything. Tokollo and I didn't really know what we were doing, but we did know what we wanted to hear.

Zwai had been given some equipment by the record label BMG (now part of Sony), who had signed him up and wanted to invest in him as a solo artist. Zwai mentioned me and Tokollo to the record label, and they basically said, 'You guys go with it.' We just thought: these guys say we must make music? Let's make music! It was like a gang mentality. We could take on the world; we knew better than anyone else in the industry. Initially we were very influenced by hip-hop. We didn't quite have that South African 'touch' yet – that thing that makes South Africans want to dance.

We put out an EP through BMG – a CD with four tracks, in a slim case. We didn't have budget for wardrobe, or stylists or anything. We went to the top of the Top Star drive-in, and used clothes I'd bought overseas, mixed and matched with our own clothes, and we took a picture that was our cover. For the first time, we had to sign contracts. I couldn't even sign my first contract because I was too young – I had to get my parents to sign on my behalf.

That EP had this song, 'Take it Eezy'. It was quite a special song. Take it easy, when things aren't going right.

And things *weren't* really going right. We didn't have jobs. We had all flunked school or left school. My parents were on my case.

The EP came out in June 1996, and I think we sold 600 copies. It was really, really bad. I remember going to a gig – we were performing right after M'du, who was one of the biggest acts. After M'du left, everyone else started leaving too. People just wanted us to get off the stage. They started throwing cans at us as they were walking away. Some people even threw bottles.

But there was this resilience. Maybe it was also arrogance. We went and did our homework. We got to know the lay of the land, sonically. We took stock: what did we do wrong? What's inside *here* and what is happening *there* was not lining up. We realised we were sort of operating in our own silo, not mixing with the rest of the industry. Once we started doing that, it was game over.

When our second EP came out in 1997, it sold 200 000 units. And that's when it all took off.

With me and Tokollo and Zwai, there was this kind of brotherhood. It made us want the best for each other. The three of us, together, were much more than any individual. When we experienced disappointment, we would take it on ourselves to make it right for the other guys.

The advantage of being in a team – especially when you *do* have something to offer – is that you all see it in each other. Failure is not the end, because you can still see the potential: these guys, independent of me, they had something special. I saw that in them, and they saw that in me. Sometimes you have to be brutally honest with yourself: do you really have the goods? Once you've done your introspection, once you've decided you do have the goods, then you have to soldier on.

The Platinum-Selling Failure

Maybe I was hypersensitive to what I perceived as criticism. I was always waiting for someone to say something that confirmed how I felt about myself: that I was an imposter, or that I was a failure. I remember going to New York City with Tokollo and Zwai to work on the masters for the TKZee Family *album. One night we went out for a few drinks. In New York it always felt like they served you a quadruple when you asked for a double. From out of nowhere, Tokollo and Zwai started accusing me of being ... not a hanger-on, but like a passenger. I'd like to think it was the Jack Daniel's talking. They had been doing all the work, they said – what had I been doing? It was the kind of thing that reared its head more than once. And that carried over into the public space. When people – fans, or whoever – used to comment about us, they would always say: flip, when those guys go solo, that Kabelo oke is stuffed.*

About the same time that TKZee's music started coming together, I started dropping out of school – not just playing rugby, but I stopped going to some of my lectures, then I stopped going to all of them. Physiology was like having to do biology all over again.

Me not going to school would find me in Diepkloof a lot of the time, hanging out with other guys who also weren't going to school. All we would do was smoke weed all day. We would meet in the morning, and that was all we did. I was slowly becoming the person I didn't want to become.

At that stage I wasn't drinking every day because I couldn't afford it. Weed was cheap. Once my music career started to take shape, then it was whatever I wanted.

If I wasn't in Diepkloof I was at Zwai's place, or Tokollo's house. Going home meant admitting I'd failed. I could hear my parents, telling me how they had 'sent me to the best schools ...'

My mom was still very supportive. But I never wanted to face my dad, because I just felt like such a disappointment to him. I think he wanted me to become more than he was, and he never got the music thing. Even five years later, after I'd sold 700 000 records, launched my own solo career, my album had just gone gold ... he still didn't support me. The PR company thought it would be a good idea to invite my parents to one of my press conferences, so they could say how proud they were of me, I guess. My mom came – moms will do anything – but my dad said no. He told me that just because he had let me do this 'thing' all these years, it didn't mean that he agreed with it. By then my life had changed. People who had always treated me a certain way had changed. I guess I thought ... now my dad will change too. But he wasn't swayed by success. I know he loved me, and he supported me in his own way. I think part of him still wanted me to go back to school. But I actually respected him for it. He was always very principled.

Before I became successful, though, there I was, hiding out at my friends' houses, or getting high in Diepkloof. Although I think, deep down, I always knew something would happen, I was just very angry at where I was, and at how it had all turned out. And I took all my anger with me out into the world. There are a lot of stories, about me, about Tokollo, about Zwai. I don't want to tell their stories – I can only tell mine – because I want to take responsibility for my part.

Of the three of us, Zwai was always the responsible one. I will call him the best of the worst, because we were young, and we didn't always behave very well back then. I think that has been fairly well-documented in the press! Zwai used to sing – he had this trio – and he was a music teacher. He worked, and he would earn money so that we could all go out and get drunk. Zwai was like our hook-up. We'd go to this bar out on the corner of Witkoppen and Main – I think it was called Morgan's. There used to be a lot of bars out there. That was literally where our career happened from: the right bars, clubs, where you could hang out with the who's who of the music industry. All the hottest stuff got played there – and was conducive to helping us find and make the sound we were looking for. After the failure of our first EP, Morgan's was the place where we could hear what everybody else was doing. All the biggest acts in the country were there, or were played there. Bongo Maffin was on the up; Boom Shaka was huge – Boom Shaka was like our target. And if they could do it, so could we.

Music wasn't the only part of the mix. There were also girls, and booze. I remember going out the one night and just mixing *everything*. I drank beer and tequila, I smoked weed. I was one of those guys who, when you didn't have money, if the person you were drinking with ordered a shooter, you would have that. If they ordered a beer, you'd get a beer. You would have whatever they were drinking, and whatever they were buying.

Eventually I went to the toilet, and staggered into a cubicle and locked the door. I can't remember if I threw up. I needed a time out. I put my head against the wall, and planned to sleep for five minutes. I wound up passing out for like five hours. One minute it was 1 am, the next thing it was 6 am. I walked out the club and all these guys were outside sweeping, cleaning up after the night before. I made my way to the parking lot and tried to sleep in some corner on the concrete, but that didn't really work, so I got up and started walking in the direction of Tokollo's house in Fourways where I was staying. I managed to ask some guy for a lift, told him where I was headed, and asked him to wake me up. Then I passed out in the car. When I woke up we were already in Randburg, and I was so pissed off – I had to get out and walk the rest of the way back, then I had to basically sneak back into Tokollo's house. I had to knock on the window to get someone to let me in. When I think of that now, it's so embarrassing.

It's easy to see these as small things, boys being boys. But it ate away at my pride. Needing Zwai, needing Tokollo, not being able to take care of myself. It didn't leave me feeling great. So of course I started drinking even more. It was all about getting to the next payday, wondering where the money would come from. Hanging out with my friends and mooching off them, borrowing money from my mom.

We only really started getting productive and making something of our music when we moved out of the back room at Zwai's place. Up until then, we were just in somebody's backyard making a noise. Sometimes the people Zwai was staying with would find us in the car, passed out.

BMG had this office space where they allowed us to set up a new studio. We were in there every single day. We'd sleep over at the offices sometimes – although the record company didn't know this. And, once we were in, we'd bring the girls and the booze there too. The record company didn't know this either (although it probably wouldn't surprise them).

We were still so wet behind the ears. The first paying gig we got was performing at the Gunston 500 in Durban. We got R6 000 – two grand a person. It was just like when my dad used to give me tuckshop money. I spent that money in a day: I bought a Tommy Hilfiger jacket, Replay jeans, nice brown boots. And I was done. The other guys were laughing at me, because they still had their money. But I got to drink and smoke their money, and I had the nice clothes to show for it.

When *Phalafala*, our second EP, came out, it exploded. Suddenly there was money available. And I was the treasurer. They trusted me with the money – the promoters would pay us in cash, and I would keep the cash and pay it out as we needed it. I started crossing over to more expensive booze, started drinking whisky. I drank a lot of Bell's, but mostly I just drank a lot. There was a lot of alcohol, because it was just too easy to get, and we were celebrating.

When our single 'Shibobo' dropped, it was even bigger. It sold over 100 000 copies in its first month. To date, it is still the fastest- and biggest-selling single ever released by a South African artist. It was quite cool, how the whole thing came about. Someone from BMG knew [footballer] Benni McCarthy's manager, and we were big fans of Benni. The World Cup was coming up, so we had this idea: why don't we try and get to work with him. The A&R guy from BMG reached out, Benni's team was keen ... We recorded our vocals in studio in South Africa, and then Zwai flew to Amsterdam, where Benni was training with his club team, to record Benni's part. We only had about five minutes to write Benni's verse because Zwai just got told he was flying off to Europe at the last minute, and we had to have the lyrics ready. When it was time to shoot photographs for the sleeve, it was a bigger challenge. The Bafana Bafana training camp wouldn't let us go and shoot Benni there. So we drove out to where they were training and hid out, incognito, around the corner, just watching them. As soon as they took a break we called Benni over – there was no styling or make-up, just a guy with a camera – and we quickly put on some BMG jackets so we looked a bit more uniform. They took the shot in front of some building, and that was it. We had our cover, and our single.

By that time I was on cloud nine. I had proven my dad wrong. I had proven all my teachers wrong. The girl who had cheated on me – she was wrong too. It was like: stuff everybody, *I* have arrived.

It took me a longer time to learn that success can also neutralise you. That real success is not only about money in your pocket – it's about prospering on all fronts. Maybe you sell a lot of records, but as a person, who are you? What do you stand for? How is your relationship with your family? Are you being honest with your friends, with your bandmates? What kept the machine going, then, was just focusing on the machine. All the stuff on the side, I didn't see it as important. Success was overwhelming, and that handicapped me. You start thinking that because you have this success, everything else should happen without effort on your part, that it is all about people reaching up to *you*. What do you mean I'm not courteous enough? Don't you know who I *am*? It's easy to expect that your success should be enough to speak for you. But you still have to be a person people want to be with.

Between the Start and the Finish

There are all these stories that you find along the route of the Comrades Marathon. I don't pay attention to most of them. For me, most of the race between the start and the finish is just flashes. There is this place called Arthur's Seat, near the halfway mark, where there are often roses growing. There's this legend that, if you take a rose and put it on the seat, you *will* make your timing split. I think I might have done it on my first run, but I've never done it since then.

Not too far from Arthur's Seat is the Comrades Wall of Honour – where, if you manage to finish the race before the cut-off time, you can have your name put on one of the rows of blocks. Finishers get a yellow tag with their name and their race number. Those people who have completed 10 Comrades get a green permanent number – and a green plaque on their brick. What I love is that they always keep extending that wall.

There is Always Something to be Grateful For

Drinking, drinking, drinking.
Weed, weed, weed.
Ecstasy.
Cocaine.
That is how I remember 1999.

During the recording of our first album we worked with someone who also used to DJ on the rave scene. The rave scene was much more progressive, from a drug perspective. One day, this guy asked me if I'd ever tried ecstasy. We were in studio when I tried it. I even remember what song we were recording. In fact, it was the whole album after that – the whole of *Halloween*. I was taking ecstasy, and it *was* ecstasy. I was just like, 'Ah, this is amazing.'

There was an arrogance that came with more money. I'm not on weed any more, I'm on ecstasy, I thought to myself. Even then, I always told myself I would never take cocaine. That was crossing some line in terms of drugs. But ecstasy was cool, because it made me feel good. And I loved the combination of ecstasy and marijuana. I would pop a pill, smoke a joint, and it was like heaven. And we made such great music.

That was how Pandora's box got opened. I'd gone there. For the first couple of days after I tried ecstasy I thought: what the hell *was* that? And then I thought: I want to go there again. So I would take ecstasy once every two days. Then once a day. Then twice a day. Then three times a day. I was also drinking, so you have to add booze to the mix. For that period I guess it's not surprising I have a pretty euphoric recall.

Even now, sometimes I think if I had just stopped at ecstasy, it could have been all good. But, of course, that wasn't how it turned out.

Halloween came out in 1998, and it was a classic of note, if I do say so myself. It really defined the sound of an era – it was a pivotal moment in South African music history.

I've always been of the conviction that kwaito is South Africa's interpretation of hip-hop, mixed in with African dance grooves. *Halloween* absolutely captured those two aspects – it was real to its hip-hop influences, it was real to its township influences, and it was real to the South African urban music influence. That had never been captured in one album. We were doing rap vocals over dance grooves, but we actually had something to say, something South Africa could find itself in. After 1994, black youth were looking for a voice. We captured the potential of what South Africa's black youth could be. You can't talk about kwaito without talking about TKZee's *Halloween*.

Then the whole deck of cards started falling apart. It all came to a head at the South African Music Awards (SAMAs). In 1999 we won an unprecedented five SAMAs – for the best kwaito album, for the best group, for the best kwaito single, for the best single, and for the best video. We were like these wonder boys. People were just starting to get a glimpse of who we were, and maybe we started showing who we really were.

That year the awards were sponsored by Chivas Regal, so there was an endless supply of good whisky on our table. I was on ecstasy, we were all drinking Chivas at the table, then going up to receive one award after the other. What it must have looked like to everyone else I can only wonder. We were on top of the world. We thought.

It was very rock and roll, so maybe that stuff you can forgive. But after the awards had ended, the night took another turn. Tokollo got accused of assaulting a woman. The following week the newspapers were full of reports about this 'night of hell' with TKZee.

At that stage, in my mind, I'm super successful. I'm taking Class-A drugs. I'm arrogant. I'm making money, or what I think is money. And I had this gang mentality, that I would defend my friends to the death. You could say nothing – *nothing* – about those two guys in my presence. I remember Tokollo getting arrested, getting taken to a jail that was down the road from Sun City. He denied it, and I believed him. To this day, I don't know what happened, but I trust his version.

But when the media wrote that stuff, that was a red flag to a bull. Who did those people think they were? With one headline, we had become Public Enemy Number One and everything we did was under scrutiny. The fights I got into would be reported on. The dumbest things always ended up in the media. I think, now, that it is what happens when your lack of character starts to catch up with you.

We thought we could take on the media. They were making money from reporting on us; we were going to use *them* – and tell them to get out of our business. That's when we wrote 'Izinja Zam' – my dogs, I'm calling all my dogs, we gonna set the dogs on you. These dogs, they don't want to see us happy. They're all in our business. It was very defensive, and very aggressive. Any rock star worth his salt has got a song like that. We started gunning for them, and they kept on coming for us.

I was still taking ecstasy all the time. That was the order of the day for me: popping pills, smoking weed, drinking.

You know, when you hear the term 'drug dealer', you always think of this dark, scary character. But my drug dealer was one of the sweetest people in the world. He would give me and my friends ecstasy, we'd chill at his house. It was like this fancy drug den in the leafy northern suburbs.

One night he came to me and he put something on the table. 'Have you tried this stuff?' he asked. It was cocaine.

You always think it is so far away from you. I always said I would never try it – all these thoughts went through my head in like a nanosecond – but now it was right in front of me. And, being the big, arrogant ponce that I was, I had cultivated my own sense of my bravado. Nothing scared me. I asked my friends if we should take it. 'Ja man, come on, what's it going to do?' they said.

He gave us the first couple of grams for free, and we were all like: what a flipping nice guy he is! And there was more the next day.

After I took coke that night, I remember driving home and thinking that I couldn't even feel it. Ecstasy was still the best. I didn't even get that high. When I did finally 'get' the high ... what it did, how it made me feel ... when I was on coke, everyone else was like four feet tall. Nothing was impossible. It made me see myself as this larger-than-life person; it made me start to think in a certain way – like I was invincible.

I always had to be clean when I was on coke. My car had to be spotless. I had to wear my best clothes. That person was only released when I was on coke. When I left TKZee, when I started a solo career, I had so much self-doubt. In a strange way, coke actually helped me – because even after I had stopped taking coke, I remembered how I'd felt on it, and it was somehow easier to bring out the person who was already in there.

But once I'd started taking cocaine, ecstasy didn't cut it any more.

I was paranoid. I wore sunglasses everywhere, even indoors; I was grinding my teeth all the time, and drinking excessively. It was a cycle of uppers and downers. I could never get drunk when I was on coke. I'd go on four-day, five-day binges, without any sleep at all. Every time I dipped a little I'd just have a few lines. I always did my drugs in private – often it was in my car – and always on top of a CD case. And the bigger the note, the better it felt. It had to be like a R200 note. When I went to clubs I was always visiting bathrooms. Towards the end I became quite careless.

I was listening to Tupac a lot. He always used to talk about MOB: 'Money Over Bitches'. Women were bitches. They were not to be trusted. They were supposed to be treated like crap, because they would love you anyway. One night some girl said something to me. I don't even know what it was, but I took offence. I took a bottle of water, in the club, in front of everyone, and poured it all over her, calling her a bitch. I was that punk.

That same night, as I was walking out the club, one of my friends had started having an argument with the cops. He shouted at me, and told me to get into the driver's seat of his car. He climbed into the passenger's seat. I put the car into first and sped away down the road. The cops started chasing us. We were in a fast car, and somehow I thought I was going to get away from the cops. I came to this T-junction, but I was flying. I tried to take a sharp left, and drove straight into a wall instead. The guys I was with, they all ran. The cops recognised who I was. I paid them off and they left me alone.

Another night, I was on ecstasy, and I had been drinking. I was driving, heading towards Sandton, tripping off my head, drunk, in my friend's 4x4. The robot went amber and I guess I floored it. And suddenly there was this pizza delivery guy on a motorbike. As I hit him, I just remember this pizza flying all over the place. I ran to a garage across the road. I had this funny notion that if you ate a lot of sugar your blood-alcohol level would go down. So there I was, trying to eat all these Bar Ones. The cops who arrived at the scene, they also recognised me. And they told me to get out. I didn't think twice, I just left. That story came back to bite me a few years later. I was at the Channel O Music Awards and there was this tap on my shoulder. 'I'm advocate so-and-so. You had an accident with my client four years ago.' All the guy wanted was for his medical bills to be paid. I hadn't ever given him a second thought. I did eventually settle the matter.

There was another story with the cops. I was hanging out at a party in Yeoville with a very famous musician. He'd just bought himself a fancy, expensive new car. We were chilling at the party and then we ran out of drugs. So we decided to go to Hillbrow.

We go in his car, we get to this garage; obviously it's Hillbrow – it's not the only drug deal going down. I think we must have phoned ahead – we knew our dealer was going to be there. I can't remember if it was my dealer or my friend's dealer – maybe it was mine, because, later, the pills were on me. Anyway, we got out the car, got the drugs, and as we got back into the car, five or six cops came out of nowhere. They stopped us, made everyone get out and empty our pockets. I had all these ecstasy pills. Five guys with guns were standing behind me. I was still thinking somehow I was going to fool them. I tried to ditch the pills, but they saw me. They arrest whoever the pills are on.

They took us all to John Vorster – Joburg Central Police Station. The guy I had been driving with, the famous musician, they told him to duck and he just left me there. I can't blame him – I would have done the same. They confiscated the drugs and told me I was going upstairs.

The cops had also recognised who I was. They told me I was stupid to be buying drugs in such a public space. There was another guy in the same room as me. They were questioning him; they wanted him to snitch on his dealer. He was busy calling his dealer from the cop office. They tried to get me to do the same thing, but I wouldn't.

Then they said that if I wanted to be released, it was going to cost me R10 000 to R15 000. There were five of them, so R3 000 each. I had the money – it wasn't even a lot of money to me. I phoned a friend and asked him to collect the cash, and to come and pick me up. He came straight from a club and arrived at the station with a whole bunch of people he had been partying with. The cops didn't like that at all. They said there were too many people, and now they were going to have to arrest me properly. They took me downstairs to charge me but they couldn't find ecstasy on their computer system. It was really odd. Maybe they were just making it up to scare me a little bit more. But, whatever the reason, they wound up not being able to charge me after all and then they didn't quite know what to do with me.

I'd been arrested at maybe 10 pm? My memories of the evening are a bit hazy, because obviously I was high most of the time; high, or coming down. By the time we'd gone through all this drama, and my friends had tried to bail me out, it must have been a little after midnight, 1 am. But the cops didn't want to let me go. So they took me with them on their raids. They drove around Hillbrow, doing proper cop stings. I was just sitting in the back; they would be jumping out the car with their guns out, running. We went on at least two or three of these excursions.

By then it was the early hours of the morning. Eventually they pulled over right behind where St John's school is. 'You've got to get this money,' one of them said to me.

The one guy came with me to my manager, and we collected the cash. And then we drove back to pay the rest of them. When I came back, when I was busy paying, one of the cops gave me half a bankie of ecstasy tablets.

The next night was one of my friends' birthdays, and I just remember dishing out all these pills at this party.

Before the cops had let me go, they had warned me that if I ever told anyone what had happened, they were going to find me and plant drugs in my car, and say it was me.

You know, I don't recognise that person. The guy bribing the cops, and having car accidents, hitting people, because I was off my head. I try to identify with that person, but it's difficult. Even as I say that, I know what that person was going through.

He was a people pleaser. That's what I see. A people pleaser. And somebody who was afraid to be great.

Did I have a conscience? It was always there, but it had become numb – because of my state of mind, because of the drugs and the booze. I got desensitised to stuff. Death was part of my life. I lost friends. As much as I really believe I still had a conscience, I was able to numb it, to silence it by remaining in an active addiction.

The same thing happened to my feelings. I 'felt' it, but ... like it was something very distant. An addict's biggest flaw is not being able to feel. At rehab, I had to actually learn how to feel. Later in life, I am able to feel disappointment, failure, success. I feel every single moment.

When I hit that pizza guy, I was more worried about how my Saturday night was going to turn out. I didn't think about him, or what happened to him after I drove off. I just left. And I never thought about him afterwards – I didn't give rocks about whether or not the guy was dead. It was all about my Saturday night.

One of the reasons I enjoyed rehab was that you had to write your life story. I had to start engaging with things. The things I had forgotten about, or numbed out. That process, that helped me a lot. You start seeing things for what they are. Sometimes you think you've run out of things to be thankful for, then something comes to the fore of your life – it jumps out of you. Gratitude. There is always something to be grateful for.

Endings and Interventions

After TKZee's first EP came out, we were struggling. We decided we would go and visit Zwai's family in Port Elizabeth. Zwai had this old Golf, and we drove down to PE from Joburg. I'd never driven further than Durban so it was a great experience, that whole 'young man coming into his own' thing. I think by that stage we had also put a nice sound system into the car. We had a sjambok that travelled with us, nicknamed 'Boet Maswietie'. I don't even know why we had it with us in the car. We were just naughty.

When I was in TKZee my life revolved around the band. We bought a house together in Cedar Lakes, and paid it off, cash. By that stage we were all ready to leave home and get our own place. This was a good home in a good suburb, and it seemed like a good investment. Our house was right on the man-made lake at the centre of the estate, and we would sit on our back porch and have sundowners. We furnished it like proper bachelors: we all had our own bedrooms, but only one of them was en suite. That was Zwai's bedroom, of course. And we all slept on futon beds because that was what we thought was cool. There was a big-screen TV and tan leather couches; all the armchairs were recliners. There was a kitchen but no one ever cooked. We'd mostly eat takeout, or make a braai. I was the best at braaiing because I made the best chakalaka. We used the fridge mainly for keeping milk and beers cold. Years later, long after we moved out, I would meet people who had lived in the estate at the same time and they would be like, 'OMG, *you guys*!' I think they thought that we were drug dealers. There were always these expensive cars parked outside – BMWs, Jaguars – and they would still be parked there late into the morning, long after everyone else had gone to work. They never saw us going to work.

The more successful we got, the less music we actually made. When we were in Zwai's back room, when we were in that office at BMG ... we made so much music. But the more drugs I did, the less productive I became. Zwai and Tokollo would always say that they were pulling their weight more than I was, and that hurt. It hurt big time. You learn to communicate with each other, over the years, and I was always so appreciative of how I had been allowed to develop in the band. We had set goals for ourselves, we wanted to get better, we wanted to *be* better. I knew what I wanted to contribute, but I don't think they knew where my thoughts lay.

I wouldn't have fights with Tokollo and Zwai. The way I recall it, I would always agree with everything Tokollo said, and I would agree with everything Zwai said. We could be best of friends, but sometimes it was the other way.

I was getting fed up with people. The constant media scrutiny was driving me mad. I was at the crescendo of my drug use. I was literally going to have to beat my way out of this thing. I got into a fight with a DJ from Yfm after hearing him threaten me on radio after something I'd done – he didn't so much threaten me as reprimand me for some bad behaviour. I heard him, and I made it a point to find him.

And then I kicked his ass. He nearly had a car accident trying to get away from me.

I thought of myself as being anti-establishment. If you questioned me, you were gonna get a beat-down. It was this gangster mentality, Tupac-influenced: 'A coward dies a thousand deaths, a soldier dies but once.' I really bought into that philosophy.

I bought myself a baseball bat. My thinking behind this was that I didn't want to get a gun. I had a two-seater car, a BMW Z3 M Coupe, and I kept the bat in the back. I only ever used it twice, but I bought it with intention: if you're going to buy a baseball bat, you must use it. You must say what you're going to do, and you must mean it.

The first time I used the bat was so stupid. It was over someone who didn't even deserve it, over something really trivial. But the bat was new. I had it. I had to use it.

We were at a music venue called 206, on Louis Botha Avenue, and there was this one guy – he was just one of those kinds of people: he shot from the hip, he spoke his mind. I don't think he intended to make malice, but that night I was drunk and I was high, and I was irritated. The next thing I knew I was outside, and he was shouting at me. I have no idea what he was saying. It could have been 'stuff you', or 'eff you'. But in my mind it was all the justification I needed, and I decided it was the perfect time to use the baseball bat. I went to my car, got the bat out, and lashed out at this guy. I was even proud of myself – because, you know, don't say you're going to do something and then not do it. The other thoughts I had, I suppressed; the ones that told me I was being really stupid, where I was still asking myself: what was that all about? I don't think I made him bleed, but I can't really remember. I think I don't want to remember.

The second time, I was at a club. I was with another musician. And we walked in, and we sat at the bar. Because of who we were, well, these girls who were sitting at the bar with these other guys started noticing us. This was at the height of my cocaine use, when I was taking between three and four grams a day. The kind of drug use that makes people step aside when you walk into a place.

Anyway, these girls started making passes at us, and I remember someone saying to me to just leave it, to move on, to show some respect to the other guys they were with. But that wasn't the kind of guy I was then. Things got a bit rowdy quite quickly. Then we were all outside, and I was running to the car, fetching my bat, running back. The guys were all out of the club now, and I had my bat in my hand. There were all these people around. I told one of my friends to go get my car, to bring it round so that after I whacked this other guy we could just get out of there. And then, without warning, this guy started panelling me. He actually broke my tooth. I remember one of my back teeth breaking. That just pressed the wrong button. I swung with my bat, and I didn't care where I made contact. All I remember after the swing was the cops being there. I got put into the back of the police van, kicking and screaming and swearing, and they took me off to the police station. I don't know how they didn't confiscate the bat.

The bat always seemed to make the press. Tokollo's dad got wind of it. I think by then he was also starting to get *gatvol* of the way I was behaving. I remember him coming over to our house, and I had literally trashed the place. A bottle of Jack Daniel's had been thrown through the big-screen TV. I remember Tokollo's dad asking me where the stupid bat was, but I don't know if he took it then. I think it eventually got confiscated when I went through customs on the way to a gig overseas. My cocaine made it through though.

Eventually my mom came to visit the house. She wanted to give me a talking to. My mom asked me straight out if I was taking drugs. I couldn't lie to her – I never could. So I just said: I am on drugs, but I'm not abusing them. And that was it. I probably got a lecture afterwards, but I didn't pay any attention to what she said.

That was the first time my mom tried an intervention. After that, she was hell-bent on getting me help. She tried so many times, I can't remember them all. There was one time when I stopped using coke for six months. I was pissed off at my mom, but I realised she was right so I stopped coke for a bit. I carried on drinking.

The last time she tried to get me to stop, she called me to meet her at the City Lodge on Peter Place. She just said I had to come, and I thought: what does my mom want *now*? And as I walked in, she was sitting with Hugh Masekela. I just thought: what has this old geezer got to teach me? I didn't know much about his own past then. I was just pissed off that they were trying to tell me what to do. I don't even remember what Bra Hugh said to me that time. I thought it was none of his business. I did not have a teachable spirit at all. My mom would always tell me she was praying for me. That people she didn't even know would come to her house and knock on the door, and tell her they were praying for her son.

That last year of my using – when we were working on our album *Trinity* – things were not working for TKZee. The year before we broke up was a struggle year. Even from the time we'd released our first EP, and things weren't going so great, I remember crying, or being drunk, and begging Tokollo and Zwai: 'Guys, if you leave then what the hell am I going to do?' And I really meant it. What was I without them? It had always been really important for me to feel like I fitted in – I needed that validation; I needed to be affirmed by what other people thought of me. Tokollo and Zwai were two individuals who always gave off the vibe that they really knew what they wanted. Being in the middle of that, I kind of felt protected in that environment. I looked up to them. I kind of fell into the role of ... a younger brother who is learning, but eager, ambitious.

Tokollo was at a place where he felt that he was carrying the band. Zwai was already doing his own thing. They both needed to express themselves in a solo capacity. And the space we were in was not a good space. The night I trashed the place – maybe there was some argument? I don't remember any more. I took out my anger on everything in those days – I also kicked out the glass in the sliding door. My foot got stuck and I was cut really badly and had to be rushed to hospital. I think we just knew it was time to move on. First Zwai moved out, then I did. Tokollo stayed on there for a few more years and eventually we sold the property.

The band never formally 'broke up'. Even today, none of us has been bold enough to say 'that is the end', because we all had such a great time, and maybe the finality of it frightens us. All of us have left the back door open. Will we work together again? Anything is possible.

There's a nice word I learned, either when I was in rehab or at church. I was taught that there is being dependent, there's being independent, and then there's inter-dependence. This is not the same as co-dependency, when you enable each other's bad behaviour. In a group, I think inter-dependence is so important. I feel that, with TKZee, we were either dependent on each other, or independent, but we never learned *inter-dependency*, allowing the individual to be in the team.

Everything was for the team, and what the team was about. I've only seen a few music outfits get this right, where individuals are allowed to shine even as part of a collective. With us it was the collective or nothing. And I think that as much as we produced incredible stuff as a collective, it also stifled us, and it contributed to the friction between us.

I've learned that trust is paramount to this when you're in a team. When someone stands out because he or she is doing something different, you've got to support that person. Because when that person shines and excels, you've got to trust it is pulling the collective forward. That trust, in itself, instils so much faith in the individual who dares to stand out. And that will come back as faith in the collective.

Solo to Sober

One moment it was the three of us – me, Tokollo, Zwai – versus everybody else. The next thing, it was just me versus everybody else. Including them. All of a sudden my partners were now my competition. Even when I'd finished my first solo album, when I had two or three big hits of my own, I would be celebrating and then I would look at the people around me and think: who are these people? Where are my guys?

I started a solo career by default. I had never, ever planned to go on my own, and I felt lost and scared. Tokollo had always been like the leader; obviously he was destined for success, because he could do this thing so easily. Zwai was the consummate musician. I was still learning.

But you only know how a dog rolls if you put it into a tight corner. My confidence and my ability were growing. Parallel to that, we had achieved so much in such a short space of time – and I *had* learned. I was writing songs on pieces of paper, on anything from the back of a till slip to a notepad, but I was shy. I wasn't telling anyone about them. The guys didn't know, because I just wasn't confident enough in my own abilities yet. I had written so much material that I'd planned to use for the band. Obviously I had written pieces before then, but that was more writing under pressure, when you had to deliver.

When I write songs it's more of a words thing first. The melody does feature, but it needs gravitas. When you're making music for *kasi*, your township lingo needs to be on point. The melody usually gets taken care of in instrumentation. That was always Zwai's forte.

I was writing all these songs, and there were a lot of producers I wanted to work with – so there was this kind of pre-production, unbeknown to anyone. When Tokollo and Zwai and I parted ways, I had to fall back on this.

Vusi Leeuw, who worked in the record company's marketing department, drove to my house one day and found me in a bit of a state. I was probably also coming down from the night before.

He asked me: 'What are you doing? These guys are carrying on with their lives. What are *you* going to do?'

I really thought that, of the three of us, I was the least likely to make it. But in that moment, I went: okay, I'll do it. And I did it even though I was scared. It was only later in life that I read that quote, from Nelson Mandela, that courage is not the absence of fear, but the mastery of it.

I called Mandla 'Spikiri' Mofokeng. I called Guffy Pilane. I called Moses Molelekwa. Thank God because of the profile TKZee had created, these guys would take my call. And they were all like: when are we working together?

Making my first solo album – what would become *Everybody Watching*, which included the single 'Pantsula 4 Life' – there were two moments that really stood out for me.

The first was when I was working with Mandla Spikiri. Mandla had said he would come into the studio with me, and that I must make sure I had a bottle of Jack Daniel's and a bottle of lime cordial. I just drank the JD; he was having JD and lime – which I found a pretty strange taste.

The sample that we were using on my song 'Pantsula 4 Life' was the same one that he had used in one of the songs he had made with his group Trompies. I was basically in heaven – here was someone that I could really work with. I remember him saying that no one was going to see this coming. The beat was going, the Jack Daniel's was flowing. I had the lyrics all prepared. I went into a booth to record vocals – I'd never done it on my own before, so this was a big step of faith – and there was Mandla, encouraging me from the other side of the studio. Getting validation from Mandla was the potion I needed to push through my insecurities, my fear of life outside the TKZee bubble. Then Mandla called Oscar from Kalawa Jazmee Records, and suddenly I had these two industry heavyweights in the studio. I was so nervous – I was really, really nervous. The fact that they were sitting there meant that I needed to make things happen. And the magic was there. As soon as Mandla had laid his hands on the keyboard and played the bassline, I knew the magic was there. We got it right in one day, in one session.

When I knew that I had something special going was when Tokollo – who was in the studio next door, working on *his* solo album – came in to listen to what we were doing. Whatever he said, the way he spoke to me confirmed that I was on to something really good. And I took that confidence forward to record most of the rest of the album.

'Pantsula 4 Life' was an interesting concept. Initially, the song was planned for TKZee. Traditionally ... well, Mandla was a pantsula. A pantsula is a person who dances. When TKZee came into the industry, we changed this. And so I was giving *my* interpretation of what a pantsula was. He was a go-getter, a take-no-nonsense kind of guy, a succeed-by-any-means-necessary guy, a hustle-by-any-means-necessary guy. That's what it meant to me.

There was that N.W.A song, 'Niggaz4Life'. The lyrics went, 'It's plain to see, you can't change me. Cause I'm gonna be a nigger for life.'

I interpreted that as: I'm going to be a hustler, I'm going to keep doing my thing for life. I was also declaring that this was who I am, and that I was going to be around for time to come – outside of the shadow of TKZee. It was my coming of age, me declaring that the pie is big, and that there was indeed a slice for me.

But I was also scared through the entire process. I kept having to push myself beyond all the self-deprecating thoughts that I would never make it without TKZee.

The second big moment during that album was when I phoned the late Moses Molelekwa. The story behind that is actually quite funny. The first time I had encountered his music was nearly a decade before, in 1994. A good friend of mine, Zandi Mlambo – she was kind of like an older sister to me – she loved African music. So I came across Moses's music through her, and I just fell in love with it.

I met Moses for the first time in about 1996 when we had just recorded our first EP. Tokollo and Zwai didn't know who he was. I had a copy of his debut album, *Finding One's Self*. I saw Moses outside CSR studios; he was on a smoke break. And I just acted like a proper fan. I walked up to him, asked him if he would please sign my CD. It wasn't even my CD – it was Zandi's, but I never gave it back!

We started to befriend Moses in late 1998, and by then he knew who we were and had struck up a great relationship with the three of us – individually, and as a group. He took us to Denmark, and we performed with him at the Roskilde Music Festival. The future just looked so bright in terms of the collaborations we were going to do. He said, 'I'd love to come work with you in studio.' And then he added, '*Wena ke batla hofa* ... something special.' Something like that. He wanted to do something really special. He couldn't find the words, but I knew.

We went to the same studio where I'd been recording 'Pantsula 4 Life' – and there was me, Moses Molelekwa, and the sound engineer Andile. And one afternoon, Moses just started playing these chords for the track 'Amasheleni'. The songs that literally take me 30 minutes to get down have always been the biggest songs ever. I really feel like you are downloading it from somewhere special. From the first time Moses hit that piano, I was like: 'Andile, you've got to record this.'

I didn't even have lyrics, but because the chords evoked such a strong feeling in me, we literally had the entire song down in 35 to 40 minutes. By that time I knew I had a really cool album. When it came out, in 2001, it did better than Zwai's or Tokollo's albums. I think people didn't expect much from me. Maybe I didn't even expect it from myself.

Of course, something else *was* happening while I was recording: I was literally going crazy. I was high, taking cocaine, drinking alcohol; I was permanently getting high or I was coming down. And when it was time to start working on my next album, I was terrified because I'd have to do it all over again.

My second solo album, *Rebel with a Cause*, was completely different; it was nothing like my first one. First of all Moses had died, and that was a really big loss. Plus, by that time I was a double-platinum artist, I didn't have to split the cheque three ways, and my drug habit was going through the roof ... so my process was a bit strange. The people I was working with - It was just like one big beer and coke fest. I was making music but nothing was coming. The songs were being put down but there was nothing special. With 'Pantsula 4 Life', I remembered the moments as very special. Danny K still says *Rebel with a Cause* was my best album though.

What was also happening in the background was that my girlfriend was losing it with me. It has taken me an even longer time to admit that drugs and alcohol weren't my only problems. I was also promiscuous. This was something I only really began to own up to when I rededicated myself to God, a few years after I had got clean. Some time towards the end of 2001 or the start of 2002, I went out on a date with this girl – even though, yes, I already had a girlfriend (who deserved much better treatment than what I gave her). We went to some comedy show together, and I was coking it up and drinking. After the show we went to some club, where I carried on drinking. I met up with a bunch of guys, and the girl eventually went home. The party moved from the club to someone's house. And there was more drinking. That was the thing with me when I was on coke: I could drink anyone under the table. I left that party, found another party, found other people to party with. On the morning of the fourth day, I finally went back to my girlfriend's house. I lay down on the bed and suddenly I couldn't breathe. My heart was racing; I was having these hectic palpitations. I remember my girlfriend calling another guy, a friend of ours who lived in the same complex, and they rushed me off to hospital. This was at like 6 am, and at that time of the morning the traffic on Witkoppen Road was back-to-back all the way. We were all panicking. Our friend decided to drive straight into oncoming traffic. He just put foot and went and – what was really amazing – we didn't meet a single car, all the way to the Sunninghill Hospital.

When I got there the doctor told me, very bluntly, that I was going to have to be *really* honest about whatever it was I was on. I told him I'd been on a three-day cocaine binge. I don't think he was very sympathetic. He told me there was nothing they could give me except oxygen; that I was just going to have to lie there and ride it out. I lay there the whole day, and was eventually discharged around 4 pm. I swore I would never get drugs again – from that particular dealer. I was convinced the drugs had been laced with something, that it had nothing to do with my multi-day binge.

I basically can't remember a lot from the beginning process of the second album. I went about trying to make this music. I wanted it to be very interesting. I was back to a strong hip-hop influence. I played around with using big brass bands. I was trying to be more experimental, musically. Mapaputsi's *Izinja* came out while I was busy recording, and I knew that would be my competition.

Then my mother did that intervention with Bra Hugh, and I stopped doing coke for six months. My personal life was falling apart, slowly but surely. My career was all that was keeping me together. I was off drugs but I was still drinking. From a production perspective I was starting to feel happier. I had guys writing brass parts for me; Zwai had really taught me a lot from a music perspective, about trying out different sounds. But in terms of commercial success, I wasn't so sure.

So I called up M'du Masilela. I was so nervous to even talk to him. We'd had this stupid beef – we'd recorded a TKZee song dissing M'du. Him and Tokollo had this issue, but Zwai and I had joined in, picking up stompies. I didn't know what M'du would say when I asked if he wanted to work with me. He just said that he'd love to.

M'du was larger than life – he was one of the biggest acts in the country. And there was little me, still not feeling worthy. In terms of kwaito, you can't talk about kwaito and not mention M'du. I was nervous because it was him. I was nervous because I didn't know him. I was nervous because I wasn't on coke, and coke was my crutch. And so what I thought was: I'm just going to buy some coke, and work with M'du. I went back on coke after six months of drug-free 'clean' time.

M'du had this great house in Sandton, he had flashy cars, he had this great studio, great equipment ... He was *the* producer of the time, and I was getting to work with him. And, just like it had happened with Moses, it was when M'du was kind of just messing around that we got the chords for 'Ayeye', which would turn into one of the biggest hits on the album. As soon as I heard those chords I knew we had it. I'd written a chorus – I didn't have the verses; that was just how I worked. You have to tell the story that leads you to the chorus. And once you have the story, a chorus, and a strong hook, it's an easy process. If I could picture people singing along, I knew I'd got it.

'Ayeye' took like an hour. I started attributing this stroke of genius to the cocaine. I thought: I just need to be on cocaine to be creative. I got properly hammered at M'du's house, but I finally got it. We got the track, and then the album was finished – or, as it turned out, *nearly* finished.

Restarting drugs was like being in heaven. I wondered what I'd been doing for the previous six months. And I got deeper into it. Towards the end, my drug use started accelerating. I started taking LSD, kat, microdots – and that was in addition to my coke, and my drinking. I started smoking mandrax – mandrax and weed, to help me sleep. When I laced my weed with mandrax, then I could go to sleep for years. Six more months like that and I would have been on heroin. If I look at my trajectory, at the kinds of drugs I took after that short break, it's not hard to see where I would have ended up. What would I *not* have taken?

It was Lucas Mahlakgane who helped me finish the album, and who helped me turn my life around.

Lucas was a record executive at another label. It was him who suggested that I work with Mandla again. I said that I didn't want to work with Mandla. That I didn't want to do the same sounds. But Lucas was firm. He just said: 'You've got to go work with Mandla.' And so I went back, and Mandla and I worked together on one last song for the album, called 'It's My House', which also ended up being the biggest song on the album. I nearly never did that song. It was another one of those classic stories – it took us 45 minutes, maybe an hour. The chorus had actually been given to me by my late friend Thuli. He told me to use it.

Lucas used to call me *motlokgolo* – nephew. One day he said to me, '*Motlokgolo*, you got your whole life ahead of you. Why don't you just stop this crap?'

For some reason I listened. I don't know why, or what it was that he said that finally got through – whether it was how he referred to me, or the words he used, or just that I was finally ready. People should never, ever stop with interventions. Never ever stop saying something. Eventually the person will crack. Or at least you will keep that person accountable. Of course, there's a catch: it only works when the person you speak to realises they need help, when they admit they have a problem, and when they ask for help. I'm often asked to intervene and, often, I say no. I put myself into the drug addict's shoes and I know exactly how he or she feels – usually, these are guys at the same level as me, in terms of their success. It's not hard to tell when a person is not going to hear what I'm saying to them right now. It was only when I had admitted that I needed help, that I was ready to listen.

I was sick and tired of the way I was living, the way I was feeling. I thought: this is *not* how my life is going to end. The thing was, I also realised I needed to clean up not only for me, but for so many of my friends. They needed to see that it was possible to live a life without drugs, without alcohol, and that it could also be a successful life.

What happened next was a bit of a whirlwind. Lucas had a lot of connections with the media, and before I knew it I was appearing on *The Felicia Show* talking about my addiction. I knew that once it was public, I would have to do something about it. My plan was to do it once, and that would be that.

I was introduced to Janine Lewin at an organisation called MAAPSA – the Musicians and Artists Assistance Programme of South Africa, which was started by Bra Hugh and which helped artists who had drug and alcohol problems, among other things. Janine told me that MAAPSA had a fund, and that they would set me up with a rehabilitation programme. She became my counsellor and helped get everything ready for me.

How supernatural is that? I didn't even have to *think* about it. Everything was just ... there, ready, waiting for me, completely taken care of. When you come to the end of yourself, you come to the beginning of what God can do. You open yourself up for help to manifest in your life.

By then I had moved out of the house in Fourways – it was way too volatile; Zwai had also moved out, and none of us were in contact with each other. I was getting a lot of support from the girl I was seeing, and she made it do-able for me. She was fed up, and had threatened to leave me if I didn't move out of the Fourways house, and clean up. It was like a new lease on life for both of us. My mom, obviously, was thrilled I was getting help. She has always been so consistent in supporting me.

I met Janine in mid-September, and we agreed that I would go into rehab on 1 November. I know it's usually a bad idea to delay going in, but I had work commitments, and Janine helped me to get clean, and to *stick* with it. I had already been completely sober for two months by the time I checked in to the in-patient facility. During that time I shot a music video for 'It's My House', and started doing publicity for the album. Of course, the media ate it up, the story of my addiction, and my plan to come clean. It definitely helped with the promotion of the album – although there were more than a few people, including some of my friends, who accused me of doing the whole thing as a publicity stunt.

Other than that, it was the most amazing time for me. For the first time I started feeling like I was in control – it was like a new day. And I felt like the whole industry really rallied behind me. Everybody was there – radio stations, TV, the record company. My album sold gold while I was in rehab, and later went double-platinum. When I came out, if I even made a joke about feeling like a drink, people would immediately get super-protective. That hasn't changed. These days I don't really make jokes about it. There is a reason for that, and it's not just about the passing of time.

Not too long ago, when I was getting ready to perform at a gig, I was standing around with all these musicians. They were drinking alcohol and I was drinking Red Bull. At one point a group of them lit a joint and started passing it around. They didn't offer it to me, of course. But inside me, my arm went and reached out for the joint. That freaked me out a lot – it frightened me that that person was still there. I just retreated, walked away, and dealt with it quietly on my own. But I was really surprised by that little voice; that, after all these years, it was still able to creep up on me. 'It's been so long, what harm could it do?' it whispers. Luckily the other voice is stronger, telling me: 'Let's not only have euphoric recall, Kabelo. Play the whole movie through.' I'm still the guy who is one drink, one drag away from my addiction.

The Hill without End

The Valley of 1 000 Hills is supposed to be one of the most beautiful places in the country. People talk about it quite romantically. But when you're running up those hills, the view counts for nothing. A few kilometres after the halfway point of the up run, you reach the longest hill: Inchanga. Oh man. Inchanga is the worst thing ever. It doesn't end. It just doesn't end. When you think it's finished ... you go over a rise and it carries on. And it's bad coming down *and* going up. This is the part of the race that has no mercy. You come out at halfway and it's so quiet. It's one of the few places where it's mostly just us runners. Nobody really stops to look at what's around them. The good runners, the strong runners, the ones who are making their splits, they are the guys who are pushing up Inchanga. Maybe they will walk for a bit, but they will always pick up the pace again.

I am the Monster

Maybe I am contributing to that myth of famous people who always get away with crap. When the Jub Jub thing came out I was very slow to point fingers, because I knew, without a shadow of a doubt, that it could have been me. Even Oscar Pistorius – every time I watched that case, my heart broke. That could also have been me, on so many levels. My temper, mixed with the drugs I was taking. Uncalculating, but angry. I hit a woman once. It was when I was stone-cold sober, had been off drugs for a couple of months. It was the most frustrated I had ever been. I don't know if, even now, I am ready to talk about this. These men we see as monsters, it's also something that can be closer than you know. You can be the monster. You just got lucky that you didn't get caught.

The first step of the Twelve-step programme is to admit that you are powerless over your addiction, and that your life has become unmanageable. Before then, my life was unmanageable. I could not manage my life. If I could, I wouldn't have been there, in that place. And it was flipping hard work. It hurt. It required real bravery to go through that process. I actually understand why a lot of people stay the way they are.

I went into rehab, as planned, on 1 November, and I came out on 13 December. Two days after that I had a gig – it was something that had been planned a lot earlier, before I even went into rehab. I remember getting on stage and the crowd going berserk. I was really appreciative of getting a second chance. I felt like I had got my self-respect back. That people would start respecting me for being honest about what I was going through. I had been like this villain, and all of a sudden I was made to feel like I was a hero.

But there were people who weren't happy with my sobriety. It said more about where they were at. I was accused of doing it as a publicity stunt, of being a media whore. Often by people who were in active addiction. For the first second, when you find out, it hurts deeply. But I had to rise above it. Everyone is entitled to their own opinion. I can't force someone to think about me in a certain way. If an orange tree says it's an orange tree, then you've got to give it time to bear some oranges. If harvest time comes and it bears apples, you will know who the imposter is. You will know me by my fruit.

My mother came to visit me at the rehab centre every weekend. She was always there for me. She didn't have to say anything; she was known by her actions. The addict goes in, but, parallel to that, the family goes through their own counselling. When I saw my mom give herself over to that, try to understand me, I knew that she was really there for me.

One of the things you have to do as part of a Twelve-step programme is write your own life story. See what kind of a prick you actually were. You have to travel down that road, start writing down all this stuff. For me, that is part of what spurs an addict on to sobriety: jeez, I did that? I didn't sign up to be this person. Then, of course, after a few weeks you have to read your story out loud, to your group. When you learn about other people's crap, you hear their stories week after week, it slowly becomes a safe environment for you to share yours. When you see someone else become transparent, it encourages you to become transparent.

When I finally read out my story, there were proud moments – because of the good stuff I had achieved – but also embarrassing moments, humbling moments. If anything, rehab humbled me. It made me realise that the sun didn't shine out of my bum, and that when I drive around at night the moon is not following me. So there was pride, and there was regret. Regret because ... if I had paid more attention and not missed so many things, I would be much further in life. As much as you pat yourself on the back after rehab, because you came out clean, you did it, part of that process is also realising how many opportunities you missed because of your addiction.

The first day I arrived at Houghton House, I was shown around, told where to go, and then thrown straight into 'group'. There were plastic chairs placed in a circle. I sat down with this kind of 'Do you know who I am?' attitude. I folded my arms – I was completely arrogant, even though by that time I was already clean; or maybe it was because of that – and I just sat and looked at these people, pretended to listen to them. Maybe I was hearing what they said, but I wasn't really listening. This one girl was sharing her story with the group. Like I said, you share where you have been so that people can identify with you and find strength in where you have been. It's kind of a sacred space. It requires a huge amount of trust.

So, she was sharing her stuff. And I decided to just chip in. I gave her advice: I think you should do this, and you should do that. This is so embarrassing when I think of it now – not just me thinking that I obviously knew better than *everyone* else, but just the complete disrespect, like I was stomping all over the stuff she was sharing. I think everyone in the group was completely horrified at my behaviour. Worse, still, I carried on acting like that for another week or so. That story about me made the rounds. And my mistake ultimately wound up being the beginning of my healing process, and me understanding what I was there to do.

A week later, when the group met and got to confront each other, or confront another addict for their conduct, or applaud someone – it didn't have to be negative – I remember basically the *whole* room just gunning for me. 'We don't know who you think you are. This is not the music industry. You are so arrogant ...' They really let me have it.

I had always had 'yes people' surrounding me – there were very few people who challenged who I was, or what I did. For the first time in my life that I could remember, there were all these people in this room, and they were *all* telling me where to get off. It was the first time that the penny dropped: that I had come there to change.

They didn't just tell me what they thought about my behaviour. People told me how I made them feel. Nobody with a conscience would want to give off what I was giving off. And that's when I started putting in the work. At the end of five weeks, the reports about me had changed. People thanked me for taking to heart what they had said about me. But it wasn't just what they'd said about me that caused that change. My headspace started to shift when I started hearing their stories, really hearing them. When you hear someone else's life story, it gives you the ability to put everything in a different context. You start to understand people more, you're able to empathise with them. The fact that some people made my mountains look like molehills ... it made me want to understand people more.

Before rehab it wasn't that I didn't notice other people – it was more that I just ignored them.

Rehab was for a period of six weeks. During the first week you can't get any phone calls, and I remember being irritated that I couldn't even take a call – I mean, I had a new album out; there was a lot on the go. You had all the guys in one side of the house, the women on another. You had to make your bed every single morning, and you were on duty every other day – cleaning the house, washing dishes. That was something I was initially not so happy about. After breakfast, you'd have group. After lunch, more group. You'd talk to your psychologist once a week. My counsellor was Juliet Smith – she was amazing, although she asked many challenging questions!

The difference between rehab and boarding school was that, at boarding school, I was never held accountable for my feelings, my behaviour. Sure, I'd be caught out every now and then and get a lashing from the head of house. But at school that made you cool; it got you accepted by the other boys. Rehab was real life – what people were going through. It was a matter of life and death. We were constantly reminded of what would happen if we carried on with our behaviour: jail, institutions, death. The stakes were higher.

I wasn't particularly physically active at the time I checked in to Houghton House – I had a rowing machine at Cedar Lakes, which I would remember to use every other month. But I'd do sit-ups and push-ups, and invite people to come over and play tennis. So the fitness was still there. When I first got to Houghton House I decided to start training. They had free weights in the garage. I would run up and down the steps, and do weights. I was told to stop doing it. Not that exercise was an addiction, but that it was a diversion – it prevented me from dealing with the issues that I was going to have to confront. I was told to stop training so that I could focus on my addiction. They did allow us to play soccer though, because it included other people, so we played lots and lots of soccer.

We had these diaries that we were expected to write in every single day – we would leave them for the counsellors to read. When you were writing your entries, you were not allowed to use the word 'fine'. They told us it stood for F-ed up, Insecure, Neurotic, Emotional. It is a good principle; it teaches you to identify how you are actually feeling – that was one of the most important lessons, to be able to identify your feelings. Another acronym they used was HALT. You must stop (what you are doing) when you are feeling: Hungry (if you're hungry, eat), Angry or Lonely (if you feel like that, try and trace back those feelings and find their origins), or Tired (if you're tired, get some sleep) – because those feelings are often triggers that will make you think, I'm feeling [this way], I'm just going to go and use again.

Tracing back emotions is still a tool I use today. When you find the root of your emotion, you are better able to deal with it and move on.

Initially I thought that the whole diary exercise was a drag. Your progress was constantly being monitored. If you weren't writing enough or expressing yourself enough, you were held to account. I thought that the stuff I needed to write, or wanted to write, wasn't the kind of stuff they were looking for. Sometimes it just felt like a drag to have to write down the things that were expected: I did cocaine there, I did cocaine here, then I was hospitalised. Writing also meant that I was supposed to be baring my soul – they wanted to know what was happening *inside* me. I wasn't accustomed to that. All those actions that I had done, slowly, they started to mean something. I started to think clearly about myself – and I realised I was actually a bit of a nasty person. I wasn't as great as I thought I was. I hadn't been honest. I hadn't been faithful to the girl I was seeing at the time. Treating her as badly as I did just kind of jumped out at me. Also my baseball bat phase. You start seeing yourself as kind of like a monster.

When you were writing in your diary you couldn't cut corners. It was being read. You had to be real, and actually say what you thought, felt. Also, every single day you had to identify five things that you were grateful for. I remember being grateful for: visits – from my girlfriend, and from my mom, and my dad; for eventually being allowed phone calls; for clean time; for finding out that my album had just sold gold. A few industry guys came to see me while I was in rehab, but I can't remember who. I think Zwai came to see me. Zwai had always been very supportive. I was closest to Tokollo, at the time before I went into rehab, but he didn't come and visit. I think a lot of my friends felt betrayed. It was a betrayal in terms of how we lived life. And if I was implicated, then it meant they were implicated too.

My dad, I think, also struggled with what this meant. He came from the old school. I don't think that, in his wildest imagination, he thought he would be dealing with a drug addict for a son. I don't think he knew how to deal with it. I would be talking with my mom, and he would just sit there, blank. When I'm faced with stuff that I can't deal with, I'm the same! My mom was completely different. She educated herself. She would come to support groups, so she could try and learn how to deal with it. She was involved, and she was very present during my active recovery. I guess my dad was just really hurt. Maybe he questioned himself as a parent. Maybe he took responsibility for it. He was a good man, and I know he thought stuff through – but he just wasn't able to engage with the rehab process beyond physically arriving at the centre, and sitting there.

You must remember, this was in 2002, not 2015. Addiction, rehab, they weren't things many black people talked about. The older generation, like my dad, they had *seen* it in their own communities, but they had to be forced to recognise it was a problem that needed to be dealt with – and one that could be dealt with. The methods treatment centres used, the language they used … they were speaking 'addictionese'. From a cultural perspective that was *not* how people had dealt with this stuff in the past. You were expected to man up, bottle it up, and fight through life.

I wasn't the only black guy in rehab, but one thing did bug me: all the material was in English. And some of the other men in there didn't get it. African culture is quite conservative. An older person – maybe even a younger person – divulging all their personal stuff in a public space … it just wouldn't happen. An elderly man will never show how he feels. I felt like that was what some of the people at rehab had to deal with, and that cultural difference wasn't taken into account – they weren't given the proper tools to work with it, or around it, and some of them left the programme early because of that. That might just have been my experience, or just the group of people I was with, or the time when we were there. Treatment programmes are constantly changing, expanding. But I think this is still a very real issue for many addicts.

Some parts of our diaries would get read aloud in the group sessions. With the help of the counsellors, it got to a point where sharing wasn't so bad any more. Also, I was hell-bent on making rehab work. We were always encouraged to give ourselves to the process. I'm allergic to failures. I was going to be the guy who was clean for 20, 30 years, longer. Every Sunday we would go to meetings in Parkhurst, real-life NA (Narcotics Anonymous) meetings. I remember the one meeting where this woman stood up. She was a beautiful woman, in her fifties. She said that she was 12 years clean. That statement caused a bit of a reaction in the room – because at that stage no one else had that much clean time. I mean, we were all still on *days*: 30 days clean, 60 days clean, 90 days clean. It was like hearing about people who have been married for 50 or 60 years. I thought to myself: I want to be like that.

One of my strengths is that I am very competitive. When I heard this woman, I was also thinking: you've been clean for 12 years, I'm going to do double that. You've been married 50 years? I'm gonna make 100. You know what I mean though. If you use your competitive nature productively, it can be a real strength.

I was very, very present throughout my rehab. They always drummed it into our heads that if you follow the principles, you will stay clean. Go to 90 meetings in 90 days, and don't miss a single day. I didn't miss one meeting. That is why I am still here, today. I gave myself to the whole process. I was arrogant when I started. The old Kabelo, he would have thought it was beneath him – to follow other people's principles. But I knew, even then – and I know it now – that if I cheated, I would be in trouble.

I hope that woman is 25 years clean now. I don't know whether she attended a lot of meetings, or if she just came that day. But she gave me hope and inspiration. I haven't been to a meeting recently – I did go, for a long while afterwards; I would go at the big milestones. But I haven't gone recently. I should go. That's something I need to do, maybe so that my story can have the same impact on someone else as that woman's did, on me. I guess, with my faith, believing in the power of confession, I've started to change my thinking. I'm not a drug addict any more. I'm a recovered addict. But I have to humble myself. Understanding what it does for other people, more than just you, that's important. A few years ago a friend of mine who was embarking on this same road asked me to come with him to one of his meetings. Being there, seeing the brokenness, and the fighting spirit to get better, it was a good reminder. Complacency is not an option.

Two days before I finished the six-week programme, there was a press conference. In the last week before you left, you could get a day pass out of the centre. The record company wanted to hold a press conference. I'd just sold gold. For them, clearly, the album was going through the roof. Like I said, it honestly felt like the whole industry had rallied behind me while I was in rehab – and, obviously, my record label capitalised on it. As much as I was kind of aware of what was going on outside, and I was planning on what to do when I got out, it was still kind of at the back of my mind. The press conference was definitely their idea, not mine! But, there I was, talking about rehab, talking about my album – all revved up. And then, when it was over, I went back to rehab.

My birthday was 15 December. It was two days after I'd come out of rehab. I turned 26, and I had this gig in Midrand in front of 5 000 people. I remember them singing 'Happy Birthday' to me, going crazy over the new album. I just felt so much love and support. I guess people were seeing themselves in me.

After I left, everything was business as normal – aside from going to meetings every day, and occasionally seeing my psychologist. I pretty much went straight into recording my new album.

One theme that comes out of what I learned from that experience is that of endurance. I'll use David in the Bible as an example. Before Goliath, David killed a lion and a bear. God gave him strength. In David's mind, by the time he got to Goliath, he knew he would be able to kill him. I see drugs, promiscuity, anger ... at one point in my life they were like the giant. But I was able to overcome one thing, and I used that knowledge to understand that I could overcome whatever I was faced with. That is endurance – it's not fitness, it's spirit. A spirit of endurance is a great attribute. When you go through life, you will hit speedbumps; you will go through stuff. You should never make a destiny-altering decision based on how you feel in one moment. This is now; it might not be the case in a year's time. You need to tell yourself: I am still willing to stand.

In the end it's about continuing to show up for life. I love this phrase from *The Richest Man Who Ever Lived*: 'creative persistence.' It's about persistence, and about taking the knocks. What I am learning now is that those knocks come ... and they come ... and they come ... My default setting is that I always work from the end, backwards. I am at the end, where triumph and victory has come to pass. I work backwards, knowing that I will reach that point. In the end I win.

The Beat Goes On

My father's given name was Alpheus, but most people called him 'Baks'. I called him Papa. When I picture him in my head, the image that comes up is this guy who is very intelligent and articulate, who loves being articulate, and who views himself as being a very principled person. Whether he was or not, my dad always gave off this aura of being a very principled man. When I was a kid I couldn't see this. We can be very selfish, as children, sometimes. I often cringe when I think of the way I treated him, or referred to him. I definitely see myself as trying to catch up with my dad, and meeting his standards.

I started recording my next album in early 2003. We recorded through April, May – the album usually comes out around September. In June that year my father passed away.

My father had been ill for a long time. He had a weak heart, which was further weakened by his asthma medication. Also, it didn't help that, for most of his life, he had abused alcohol. In the final months there was a procession of days my dad was in and out of hospital. You kind of get prepared. He had started using an oxygen machine at home. My sister says that I was very fortunate, to be away from home during this time, because they had to see Dad deteriorate in real time and I didn't. She was very young when she said that, and it was quite profound.

My mother and I have slightly different memories of the day my father died. I don't know if going through life and remembering things a certain way helps you deal with them differently? It's also not always important which memory is 'correct'.

On the day my dad died, I had rushed to go and see him at the hospital – he was at the Lesedi Clinic in Soweto. Talking about this day with my mother helped me remember one quite awesome detail, which I had forgotten. While my dad was lying there, he asked me if I was okay – 'Are you fine?' was what he said. And I was actually in a bit of a hurry, because I had been there for a while, and the last few days I had been back and forth to the clinic. And then he said: '*O tla ja masepa a thaka tsa gao.*' Basically: that I needed to get my act together and focus on what I was doing. Because if I didn't, my peers would 'shit all over my face'. My mom said it was like his last pep talk. I didn't realise he was saying goodbye.

As soon as I got home, I got a phone call telling me that I had to come back. My dad's heart had stopped for a lengthy period of time. They kept having to resuscitate him. His heart had stopped for long enough that it could mean brain damage.

My mom was at the clinic, and my aunt, my dad's older sister, was with her. That was what faced us, the knowledge that my dad's heart had stopped, that there was a chance he would be brain dead. We had to make a decision. My mom passed the responsibility to my aunt, and my aunt passed the responsibility on to me. I don't know why my mom did that. Then my aunt was saying, 'It's not my decision, it's his,' meaning me.

All I could picture was my dad, this very opinionated man of conviction. I tried to imagine him being brain damaged, being disabled, having to take care of him. I could see him saying: I'm not having any of that.

My dad was always so alive. When he was there, he was *there*. And I knew what he would have said to me. Just let me go please. He said something else to me that day. I keep trying to think what it was, exactly. He didn't do the whole 'take care of your mother and brother and sister'. He said, 'I'm going,' or, 'I want to go.' Something like that. With my mom, he gave her instructions – go there, do that, sell the house, this is my policy number ... Apparently he thanked her. And he started singing, '*Koloi ya Eliya, ha e duma ke a tsamaya*.' Elijah's chariot. When it roars, it's time for me to leave.

I told the doctors that they had to switch the machines off, and they did.

It's a classic case of the older I get the more wise my dad becomes. My issues with my dad stemmed from the on-off tension between him and my mother. As the first-born son, naturally I was very overprotective of my mother. And I misunderstood my father's desires for me as him trying to stifle whatever dreams and aspirations I had – only to discover, later, that he always had my best interests at heart. It was just a massive communication breakdown. He spoke at a frequency that I couldn't decode. When I cleaned up, I could see it more clearly. One thing I learned in rehab was that your parents will always be your parents. I embraced that. And, as I changed, I started to see my dad in this new light. Nothing had changed about *him*; he was exactly the same as he had always been. But what changed was when he saw *I* had changed with him. I started to look forward to going home. If I was at home and we were in the room together, I would engage with him. Being in that frame of mind, receiving what he was saying with the intention of applying it, that felt good. It was very short-lived but it was all I needed. I do think about him, particularly with the birth of my daughter, with certain milestones and experiences. If he was here he'd be beside himself with happiness.

I named my next album *And the Beat Goes On*, because even though my dad had passed, the beat still had to go on.

I had gone into the new album not being on drugs, not on alcohol, completely clean and sober. My songwriting process was still the same as it always had been: I still started from the foundation that you have to have a strong chorus. My MO was also the same. The lyrics had to be weighty. It had to feel as if you were saying something. I guess ... by that time, I also felt like I was being looked at as someone who thought about what they were going to say, and that was important to me. Whether it was inspirational stuff, or shallow party music, I wanted to be seen as someone who had started to think things through before they said something.

I was still writing all these verses, telling my story in the verses; I was still working with the hottest producers. Nobody changed their behaviour with me now that I was sober – maybe they became a little more protective with me. And, also, maybe a little more open. The people I worked with, those who drank, or who smoked weed, or more – suddenly these people found the need to tell me they were struggling with alcohol, or with drugs.

At the same time, I was still too caught up with what I thought of as being the 'best'. And, gradually, this started to have an impact on the music that I was making.

My third album was my biggest seller to date. The track 'Zonke' was another one of those under-an-hour magic moments. With 'Zonke' I felt like – oh my God, I did it again! I must obviously have this 'thing', this X-factor. I was thinking – I still believe this – that there is a vault of songs, in heaven. And we need to tap into a certain place in our lives before we can download from this vault. My biggest songs all happened like that; so, for me, it shows that there has to be a bigger being out there. Mafikizolo's 'Happiness', Sting's 'Fragile', Michael Jackson's 'The Girl is Mine', Pharrell's 'Happy' ... those songs are from somewhere. I believe it is impossible for mere humans to have come up with such brilliance.

I know, especially in the final days of my drug use, how insecure I was. Going into the studio, laying down vocals – it was a big challenge. You have to open yourself up, and become vulnerable. And when the special moments happen, they happen because they come from someone else. When that moment happened with 'Zonke', I guess it crossed my mind that maybe that 'somewhere else' wasn't the drugs but that those songs, the great songs, were out there, waiting to be accessed, waiting to be downloaded. I have actually surrendered myself to that process. When I wrote the song 'Dubula Dubula', from the album *Exodus*, it came to me while I was brushing my teeth! But it wasn't completely out of nowhere. I had been singing the whole morning. I was getting myself into that space where I was ready to download the song. Sometimes I get melodies, and think I'm going to remember them later but I don't. You hear things on another frequency. You know when that frequency is active. These days, I will even pull over onto the side of the road to write something down when it comes to me.

For an album to become a phenomenon it takes a combination of factors. If you look at Michael Jackson's *Thriller* – the album was good, the songs were spectacular, and it was also released at the birth of MTV. All those things played a role in making it the success that it was. It was the same for TKZee – after our first EP, our songs were really good, we had a different sound, and it was around the start of Yfm, so we had a station that made our music accessible to a much larger audience.

By the time I made my third album I was this poster boy for sobriety – and that support made a big difference, personally and professionally – but the crossover between the social aspect of who I was, and what I was trying to achieve professionally, meant I started prioritising too many things that weren't about the music. My first two albums, for me, were really about the music – I loved the music. The fact that I could stand on my own, outside TKZee, and still make great music, it meant a lot to me. But I got too caught up in building my brand; I got too comfortable. The same thing had happened with TKZee, too, to some extent. When the commercial element starts to come in – the success, the awards – that stuff starts to matter more than anything else. I was releasing albums to win – but the music lost. The emphasis became about other things: endorsements, media appearances. It was great because you earned money; there were suddenly different revenue streams. But the art ... that suffered.

And I really felt it when I released my fourth album. My revenue streams started dwindling too. It's funny how, when the focus moves away from the music, all those other nice fancy things also start to suffer. People said they liked the Kabelo who was on drugs. That he made good music. But it wasn't the drugs. It was me. On my fourth album, I didn't know what I was doing. I got so caught up in competing, I wasn't watching my race. The music landscape was changing right under my nose and I didn't even notice it. The sound had changed; kwaito, in the form that we knew it, was changing.

I was also at a very confusing juncture in my life. In 2004, I was walking this fine line. I had rededicated my life to Christ. I was at a stage where I wanted to do what was right, and I wanted to be true to my faith – but I had this battle of the worlds. I was a secular musician, but at the same time I was a Christian. I didn't know how to marry the two. It was quite a radical time. I spoke about my faith everywhere that I went. I was such an advocate for believing; I really believed. I was celebrating my faith: he who has been forgiven much rejoices much. But I was struggling. My music was all about being hardcore, about life in the townships, about making money. It was very secular and not conscious at all. It was all good times, making feel-good music. I think my outward faith really affected my standing in the secular music industry. Even someone like Oprah – of late, she has become very open about her relationship with God. But, for most of her career, she just went about quietly and did her thing. It was only at a certain time that she came out, and talked about her faith in Jesus.

Sometimes I think I wish I had done that. Sometimes. I also felt quite isolated. I'm sure there were people I could speak to, but I didn't have the presence of mind. I was alone in this struggle, and it opened me up to ridicule. With this, I must thank my pastor Ray McCauley. Eventually I went to him and I said, flip, this thing is really messing me up. And he said: 'Kabelo, you're not a pastor. You are a rock and roll singer who is in love with Jesus Christ.' He calls it like that, rock and roll. Pastor Ray is my spiritual father; he speaks into my life. He has walked the road with me. I wish I had gone to him earlier.

When I rededicated myself to God, I decided I was sick and tired of picking up Bible story stompies; I wanted to learn the Bible for myself. So I went to Bible school, full-time, every day, for three years. When I graduated the media was there. I remember doing an interview and this guy asked me if I was a pastor, and I made some offhand comment like ... well, if I *do* get called one day ... The next thing, it was on the front page of the *Sunday World*: 'From pantsula to pastor'. Then every time people write about me, it's Pastor Mabalane. People just put me into a box. I went to Bible school, but I'm not a pastor. However, if the time does come for me to go into the ministry full-time, then I will.

I started another band, Blackjack, working with up-and-coming musicians. I was going to use the band as a conduit to do more inspirational music – I wasn't going to do this hardcore kwaito any more. I released another album. But it didn't work commercially. My sales were starting to dwindle. So I went back to how I used to do things; I made another album – and, thankfully, I still had 'it'. It worked. I could still make music people wanted to listen to. But I couldn't shake off this whole 'pastor' thing. And that drove me nuts.

I never used to be calculating when I was on drugs. I was the kind of guy who wore my heart on my sleeve. Being sober, I became very calculating. I was very cognisant of where I had been, and where I was at. I didn't want people to think of me as just a pastor. I wasn't ashamed of my faith, but I didn't want to be defined as that. I've since made peace with the fact that my identity lies in my faith. At that time, because of a lack of experience, a lack of knowledge and wisdom, I hadn't made peace with it. Now I am quite unapologetic about it. Then, I tried to make excuses, I tried to make people happy. I finally realised that when *I* became comfortable with who I was, people would become comfortable with me.

My ... whether you want to call it a lack of calculation, or just being naive, whatever that was, it came back to haunt me in other ways. Between 2006 and 2010, the South African Revenue Service

(SARS) came after me for tax sins I had committed in the 1990s, when I was with TKZee. SARS wasn't really that active in our industry when we started. Then SARS went back and did a big recon ... and found out we hadn't complied. When I was 21 or 22 I vaguely remember someone from the record company talking about paying tax, but I never really paid attention. I wish that, when I had signed as an independent contractor, tax had been docked automatically, and paid directly over to SARS.

In 2006 Zwai, Tokollo and I were presented with this massive tax bill. My share alone was close to R1.8 million. And that was at a time when my record sales had gone down, and I was struggling with the dichotomy of the person I was trying to be. I was still performing regularly, but not as frequently as I was accustomed to. And SARS came knocking. Every cent that I earned. My cellphone deals, money, income from shows, sponsorships, I had to show everything to them. I couldn't account for what had been spent where, I couldn't justify a lot of my expenses. I had to pay for my tax bill with the money I was making at the time, which put me into a really tough situation. SARS would raid my home, as if I was hiding money somewhere. I'd always driven nice cars but, to be honest, I think most of it had gone on drugs. My R2-million drug habit. It was only at the beginning of 2014 that I finally settled my account with them.

Maybe it's not surprising, with all the different things that were going on in my life, trying to juggle so many balls, that some of them were getting dropped. I think that people who knew about, say, my addiction, assumed that outside of that everything else was easy, that everything else was always going well. I do think it's important to present yourself in a certain way in the public space. When you're in public it's work, it's business as usual. I don't try and bring my personal life into that space too much. But, even at the same time as you've got to 'put your best foot forward', you also have to be brutally honest with yourself about where *you* are. Your persona – the person you are projecting in public – must never become more important than the real person. And, while you are busy interacting with people, you must remember that everybody is carrying their own cross. Some people have a way of pulling themselves towards themselves. They always look good. When you run a Comrades Marathon, by the time you hit 60 kilometres everyone is in pain; but you look around, and a lot of the people ... they *look* okay. The day I realised they weren't actually cruising, that it was hard for them, that it hurt for them too, I became a better runner.

A Rock and Roll Singer Who Loves Jesus Christ

> *When we still used to live in Pimville I used to go to St Peter Claver with some of my friends – a few of them were altar boys. They got to hand out the communion and wear these robes, and do the whole smoke and incense thing. Even though we weren't Catholic I remember thinking it was so cool. I decided I wanted to become an altar boy too. The problem was, to do that meant I would also have to go to church during the week. I wasn't interested in the process. I only wanted to wear the robes and do the whole smoke thing. So I quit, and I never set foot in that church again. It wasn't for me, then. I just wanted to wear the robes on a Sunday.*

My mom grew up in the Methodist Church – it's the church she still goes to, the church where she got married, where we all got baptised, where we had my dad's funeral – but we didn't go every Sunday. We weren't what you would call a 'church-going family'. My grandmother used to drink and smoke. Sometimes she'd take me to her friends' houses, where they would drink together. They would drink until they got happy, just on the verge of being drunk.

Then my gran went through this huge transformation. I think I walked *in* on the transformation. One day I was walking through her house, and I saw her taking her cigarettes, cutting them in half, destroying the pack. She said to me that she was chopping off the snake's head. From that day on she stopped drinking, stopped smoking, and she read the Bible every single night. She still didn't go to church every Sunday though – we would go during Lent, Easter, Christmas – but she would talk about reverence in God, reverence in prayer. It was through her that I learned the fear of God. I learned that there *was* a God. Intentionally or not, my gran drilled it into my head.

I also received a religious education, from primary school until I finished matric. Mayfair Convent was a Catholic school, so we would pray every morning at assembly. The main passage at school had this big statue of St Mary, with a little pool of holy water beneath it. You would dip your hand in the water every time you walked past it. It always gave me the sense that religion was ... not scary, but powerful. By the time I was in Standard 3 or 4 (Grade 5 or 6), I had started taking it upon myself to pray on my own. I can remember kneeling next to my bed and praying, but I have no idea what I prayed about. The only time I ever remember praying for something specific was when I was on a three-night coke binge, and I was at this club – I hadn't slept for three days, it was the middle of the week. I went into the bathroom and into one of the toilet cubicles and I sat down and I prayed that I would just get home safely. I was so high.

St Stithians was a Methodist school. The boarders would go to chapel every Sunday evening, where the reverend would speak and we would sing hymns. 'Guide Me Oh Thou Great Jehovah' was one of my favourites, because of the melody. Later on in life, when I realised what I was actually saying, it completely blew me away. But, then, it was the effect of 600 boys all singing together, the melodies and the acoustics of the chapel. If you had asked me about my religion I wouldn't have called myself anything. I was too clever for my own boots, so I probably would have answered with something like: 'What is religion? Religion is an institution.'

There were two people I knew in high school who were overtly Christian. One of them was a guy called Michael. He would talk about God, about how behaviour and speech was important. He didn't swear. I actually agreed with what he said but, typically, in those settings, you tease that person. Michael always stuck to his guns, and he was never self-righteous. The other person was Zwai. He had started off singing gospel, and he used to play me his music and talk about God, about God being active in someone's life. It made me feel better to listen to what they had to say, but I didn't honestly pay that much attention.

The first time I went to church after school was after we'd already started TKZee. I was drunk from the night before, and I was staying in Zwai's back room. That Sunday he decided he would go to church. And when you are staying at someone's house and they decide to go to church, that's what you do. So off we went to Rhema Bible Church. Before we left I rolled myself a joint, so I could smoke it after we were done.

Whoever was preaching that morning, their message made its way through to me. I knew I needed to change, I needed to stop drinking, change my lifestyle. We were called to be better, and I wanted to be better. When we got into the car after the service I threw the joint out the window.

But I didn't understand what being 'born again' meant. I thought it was like a list. If I got it right, I would be accepted. It was only later on that I realised, God accepts you, regardless. It's not about getting better first and then coming to God. It's about coming to God as you are, and He makes you better.

So that night, after spending the afternoon with my thoughts, I figured, oh well, this doesn't work, and I went back to my old ways.

But life was never quite the same after that. I believe the Holy Spirit resides in you, and it's growing all the time, telling you: I do love you, as you are. But you silence that voice. And to quieten that voice, I ramped up my intake of alcohol. Pastor Ray had a group of young adults from Rhema who would specifically reach out to people in the entertainment industry. Usually the church turns its back on people who are in the secular world. He never did. Pastor Ray would have nights at his house where he would invite people and minister to them. I went to one of these – I was as high as a kite, and he could tell. He still reminds me about it, and reminds me how far I have come.

The next time I went to church was nearly six years later, in 2002 – the week before I went into rehab. Because the substances were no longer pushing down that voice, the first thing I felt I needed to do was to rededicate my life to God. My whole family came with me to Rhema, and I went forward and I received Jesus as my Lord and Saviour.

From a spiritual perspective, I really believe I got delivered from alcohol, from addiction, from smoking. But I kind of left the back door open. In rehab, they say you deal with *everything* – and you leave this 'one thing'. Mine was promiscuity. Sleeping around. I was clean from drugs but it was the same principle. Whatever you find outside yourself that needs to fill some sort of void. I stopped going to church again. Eventually I found myself at the end of myself, again. I also messed up a really good relationship. And I thought, if

I had messed that up, and messed up big, I needed some help. The only person I felt I could turn to was God. I was sick and tired of being sick and tired. It was drugs, promiscuity ... what was going to be next? I wasn't enjoying my success, or all the scrutiny that came with it.

In 2004 I went back to Rhema Church. I rededicated my life, again. And I understood, for the first time, that it was about failing forward. You will fall, you will fail, but fall forward.

What I found was that, when you are at the end of yourself, you discover there are many others like you, who are also at the end of themselves. We are all the same, we are all in need of help.

Rhema was a big church, and there were a lot of young adults – people who were also professionals, who were also on a journey of discovery. Some of them would host 'home cells' every week, where we could meet up with like-minded people. I had a connection, with the congregation, with my peers, and with my pastor, Ray McCauley. In 2005 I decided to sign up for Bible school. At first I was just planning on doing one of the short courses at the Rhema Bible College, but when I went to register the lady behind the counter said to me: 'How awesome would it be to sit under the word of God every day of the week?' So I signed up to study full-time, Monday to Friday, every evening of the week, for three years.

I got given a set of modules, had to go and buy files and stationery ... it was a bit like going back to school. But, when the classes started, I knew that this was exactly what I had been waiting for my whole life. The words *were* life. In one of the modules, we looked at faith and character. How your character needed to keep you where your gifts took you. I was successful as a musician, but what was failing me? My character was failing me.

People didn't know what to make of my studies. They thought maybe I was a fanatic. Or that it wouldn't last. They would try and poke holes in what I was doing. I just hid out at Bible school and threw myself into the Word. The only time I engaged with the rest of the world was through my music. My phone used to ring right through the night. Suddenly my phone stopped buzzing at about 8 pm.

It didn't trouble me. I was just being bowled over by unconditional love. I was completely sold. I went to every single church conference, because I wanted to hear more. I loved the stories, the allegorical teachings, the spiritual meanings. It wasn't about some big dude in the sky waiting to whack us with a big stick.

I got caught up in research for my assignments. I also became an usher at the church because I felt that it was one thing, learning, but that you also had to *do*. And that even that was not what justified you. You were justified because God loved you, and that was it.

The best part was the follow-through that I had at Bible school. I'd always believed I was stupid and academically challenged. But I applied myself and, three years later, I graduated from the ministerial programme. The whole church was there for the graduation ceremony and I finally felt, wow, I'm actually not stupid!

As I've mentioned before, the press tried to make out like I was suddenly a pastor – they called me 'Pastor Mabalane'. But Bible school was for my own personal spiritual growth. I needed to know God for me. You can't rely on other people's relationship with God. Leading, ministering, is also not about position; it's about service. You know, David tended sheep. And he was quite faithful with that. When Samuel went to anoint one of Jesse's sons as king, it was the shepherd out in the field who God had chosen. The litmus test is, how well do you do in serving people? Leadership is about function, not position.

I carried on working as an usher, and eventually I started a home cell at my own house, especially for people in the entertainment industry – an environment where people as big as I was, bigger than me, could be themselves, could ask questions. This was how I met my wife Gail – at one of these meetings. She was already born again, and had recently moved to Johannesburg.

Speaking about my faith helps me to keep it. Do I get it right all the time? No. But it's not about my 'performance'. I guess I have had a constant battle with how this – my faith – can live parallel to my secular life. It's something I'm still figuring out, but that I want to stay true to – because the fact is, I am very passionate about my music, *and* I'm a very passionate Christian. In Acts 17:28 it says, 'For in Him we live and move, and have our being.' It's all in Him, and it will all get worked out as and when. I'm going to be who I am, and let that unfold, and ask God to teach me. I've found so much freedom in that concept. My walk is my walk – you are not responsible for my walk; you are responsible for your walk.

Proverbs 18:16 says that a 'man's gift makes room for him, and brings him before great men'. I believe this life, my music, is a gift that God has given me. So is my faith. I will never take that for granted.

Conversations with Myself

The Comrades Marathon has six cut-off points between the start and the finish. If you haven't reached the cut-off marker by a certain time, it means you're not likely to finish the race within the maximum 12 hours. On TV everybody always watches that last batch of runners coming through, those who just miss the 12-hour cut-off – who don't cross the finish line before the firing of the gun.

On an up run, the final cut-off point before the finish is at Polly Shortts, the last of the Big Five hills. This description is a bit deceptive, because you've basically been climbing since you crossed the start line. Just before Polly Shortts is another, smaller rise that they call 'Little Pollys'. It sounds cute, but it's not. I've seen people blow their race here. This is where you really have to hope your mind keeps you going, because your body no longer wants to. Your body is telling you to quit, telling you it's not worth it. When you reach Little Pollys you have to have proper conversations with yourself. Even though I am hurting by that stage of the race, it always forces me to do proper introspection. And that psyches me up.

By the time I reach Polly Shortts I know how my race is going to finish. It's less than 10 kilometres from the end, my body is warm, and the goal I have been chasing is so close. I never get fazed by Polly Shortts. For me it's a 'breeze' to push through. Most people walk it, but I run-walk, and with that consistency I pass probably 200 people on the way up. That gives me even more confidence.

During Comrades I usually stop listening to music after the halfway mark because, after that stage, I am in too much pain to draw any energy from my sounds. But when I've cleared Polly Shortts, I can actually start enjoying music again. The crowds start building up, which boosts the spirit and my mood. And I put on the beats that will take me home.

My Big Belly Day

I had checked out of rehab at the end of 2002. Between the launches of my second and fourth solo albums, I was just busy staying clean, and I was touring and performing, eating whatever I liked on the road. I put on weight so gradually that I didn't really notice it until, one morning in 2004, I sat down on my bed and I literally couldn't tie my shoelaces. Usually I could just take a deep breath, I would suck in my gut, and then I would manage to get down. And suddenly I couldn't. It was a summer's day. I had just got out the shower, but I was already sweating. I was hot, bothered, and really uncomfortable. For the first time in my life I felt like I didn't fit in my own body, and I knew I needed to change that.

On my 'big belly day' I think I weighed just a little over 110 kilograms – this is a guess, because I didn't weigh myself at the time; I only looked at my weight quite a bit later when I had slimmed down to 96 kilograms. My manager at the time had been talking about speaking to Reebok and doing some sports deal – for clothing, not exercise. The year before, Reebok had inked similar deals with Jay Z and 50 Cent. We thought: they have a South African office, why not have a local version? We went to meet with them and they actually agreed. So there was a whole shoe line, apparel, everything, all made by Reebok.

But I didn't immediately go: I designed a sports shoe, let me run the Comrades Marathon.

At some point in the previous two years, I had got a personal trainer. At the end of each session, I would try and run for five minutes on the treadmill. I remember just looking at the clock, seeing it said I had only done three minutes and 50-something seconds, and I was already almost dead.

At one point I even took the very foolish step of going onto steroids – on the advice of another trainer. I knew I needed to lose weight, and I wanted to improve my performance. The trainer said steroids would help me get stronger, and replace fat with muscle. He told me where to go to buy the stuff; there was a chemist in Joburg where it was easily available.

It took four months before I realised I was seriously not well-informed, and I had heard enough bad stuff about steroids to figure out they weren't good for me. I stopped. I switched trainers. I moved house, and changed gyms. My new trainer was clean, and didn't subscribe to any of that kind of thing. Of course, coming off steroids I put on even more weight. But I kept on training and, gradually, the five minutes on the treadmill turned to seven, then 10 minutes. Then the trainer started making me run the hill outside the gym – I had to run up, and walk down.

My big belly day actually happened somewhere in the middle of this, because, all the while, I was still eating mostly crap ... I was on the road a lot; I didn't think about what I ate before or after gigs. I had a sweet tooth deluxe. I was fat, but I was also clean and happy.

When the Reebok deal took off I wound up spending a lot of time at their head office in Durban, and I made friends with their marketing manager, Dave Turnbull. So we were touring the country, promoting the shoes and the clothing line. I was still huge. And one day, one of the conversations between Dave and me – I don't know whether he said it, or I said it, and I don't know why either of us would even have thought about doing this ... but the next thing I knew, he asked why didn't I run the Comrades Marathon.

Reebok were sponsors of the Harmony Gold Athletic Club, which was run by Nick Bester. I started thinking it would be nice to do a whole media thing, raise money for charity – get Harmony Gold to donate money for every kilometre I ran. It would also incentivise me, running for a purpose. And the next thing I knew, I was signed up.

I think that, like a lot of people, the Comrades Marathon had always been a dream. I was more of a Bruce Fordyce man – to be honest, I wasn't even sure I liked Nick Bester for beating Bruce back in 1991. I had watched every single one of Bruce's nine wins on TV. The race was one of two sporting events I would watch with my gran – Comrades and Wimbledon. She loved Wimbledon. Her favourite player was Chris Evert. She hated Martina Navratilova. We were both big Ivan Lendl fans.

At that stage I was just running those hills outside gym. I don't think I'd even clocked a kilometre on a road. I remember when I marked out how far a kilometre was for the first time, I thought: *this is quite far.*

But that's the thing about me – I like to believe it's a strength – the impossible is where my stuff is. It's always fun to take down the giants in my life.

When I told my friends, most of them said I was mad, or that I'd never be able to do it. I got a bit of a kick out of their reactions.

Nick Bester was a bit more restrained when I finally got to meet him. He must have been wondering, who the hell is this oke? I was busy thinking I would get to train with Nick Bester like every day, that he would be coaching me. What he did to 'coach' me was send me a list of dates – I think maybe he even faxed them to me – of the weekly distances I would need to run before my first marathon in March the following year. And that was the last I heard from Nick Bester for the next few months!

But I was lucky. I had the best shoes, I had all the running gear, and I had a lot of support. My on-off girlfriend bought me an iPod, and that helped my running in leaps and bounds. It literally changed my life. I loaded it with Jay Z, Beyoncé, Lenny Kravitz – when 'Fly Away' came on I just used to move! And Tokollo's stuff – that also got me going. But I still had to do the hard yards.

Before Nick had given me my first running programme, he told me that I had to be able to run 10 kilometres in under an hour before he'd talk to me again. So I chased that goal. I drove a 10-kilometre route around where I lived, and another route around my girlfriend's house. By that stage I'd moved away from my trainer; I think I had just outgrown that personal-trainer space.

I had a heart-rate monitor, but it kept on beeping all the time, so I took off the belt and just kept the watch. I think it was beeping every time I moved out of my indicated heart-rate zone, telling me to slow down. And I didn't want to slow down.

The first time I did 10 kilometres I just ran. It took me a little over an hour and 10 minutes. Before that, the longest I'd ever run was 15 minutes on a treadmill. But I'd been a tennis player, a rugby player. I *did* have an athletic bone in my body. I knew what hauling ass meant.

I used to drive the route before I ran it, and leave water bottles for myself along the way. I would go running right in the middle of the day, because I just thought that was what time people went running. So, of course, by the time I got to my bottles they would all be really hot. The distance was long, and really hard for me. I listened to music the entire time I ran, and I think I looked forward to that more than to the run.

I started running 10 kilometres once a week, usually on a Sunday. Then it increased, to three, maybe four times a week. It didn't take long to get my time under an hour. I remember cracking 58 minutes was huge for me – I would be motoring to make that time; I would be at my max, and it would only happen on good days. I told Nick about it, but I don't really think he could relate. It's something I have made peace with. Nick is an elite athlete. When you phone him jumping up and down about your 58 minutes, he's not going to go 'wow'. For him, 58 minutes is an *appalling* time. I think the only time I ever got a reaction from Nick was almost seven years later, when I ran a marathon in three hours and seven minutes. He asked me what time I'd run, and when I told him, he turned and looked at me and said: 'Genuine?'

After I'd managed to finish 10 kilometres in under an hour, my next goal was to run the Akasia 3-in-1 Marathon as my Comrades qualifier. In order to be eligible to run the Comrades, entrants have to qualify by completing a recognised marathon (that is, 42.2 kilometres), in five hours or less. Nick said Akasia was a flat and easy qualifier, a double lap of 21 kilometres. Suddenly the running programme he sent me jumped from 10 kilometres to 15 kilometres, 18 kilometres. I got a really cool 18-kilometre course by my house. I only really started enjoying it as I got fitter and better.

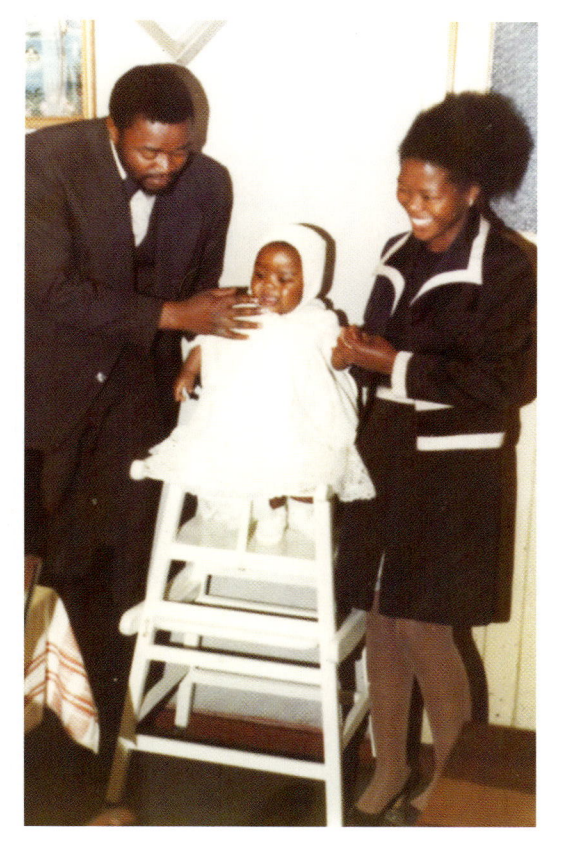

TOP LEFT: A photoshoot on my parents' wedding day, 26 May 1979.

TOP RIGHT: A week after my parents' white wedding, at the traditional ceremony in Mabaalstad.

LEFT: On my favourite high chair at my gran's house for my baptismal party, July 1977.

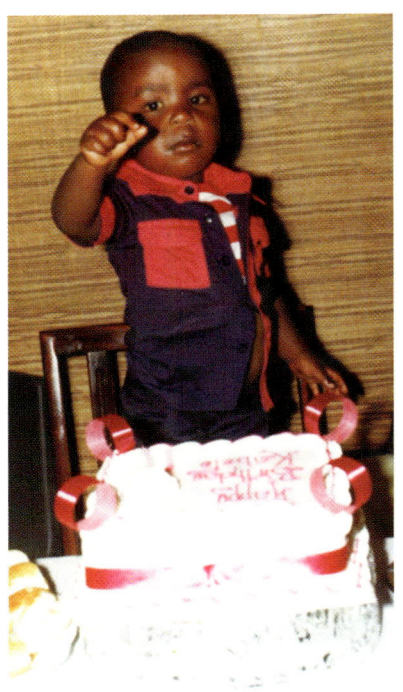

TOP: A change of clothing after the baptismal and chilling with my mom in my gran's garden.

RIGHT: My first birthday party at my gran's house, 15 December 1977. My Uncle Dan had just been sent to Robben Island – and I knew how to do a Black Power salute.

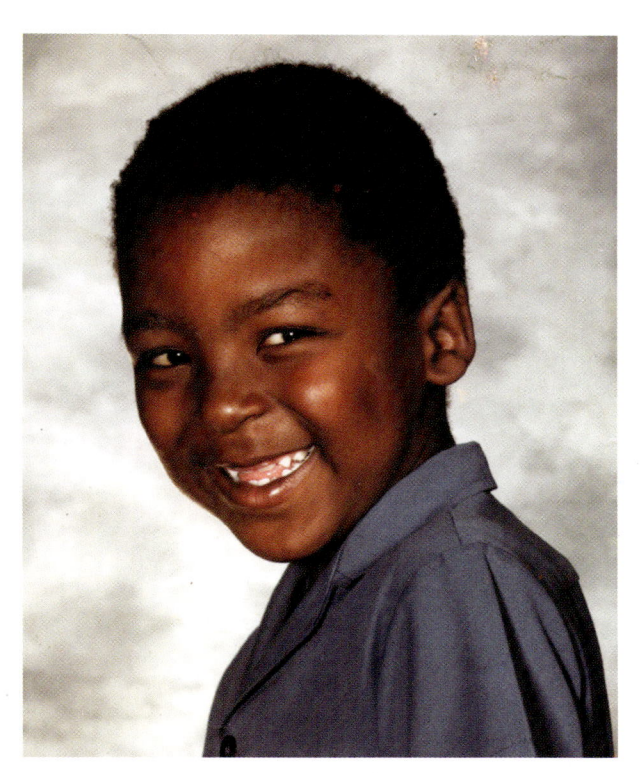

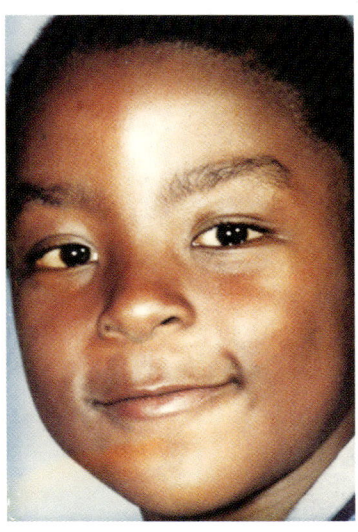

TOP: In Grade 1 at Mayfair Convent, 1983.

LEFT: An older me at Mayfair Convent.

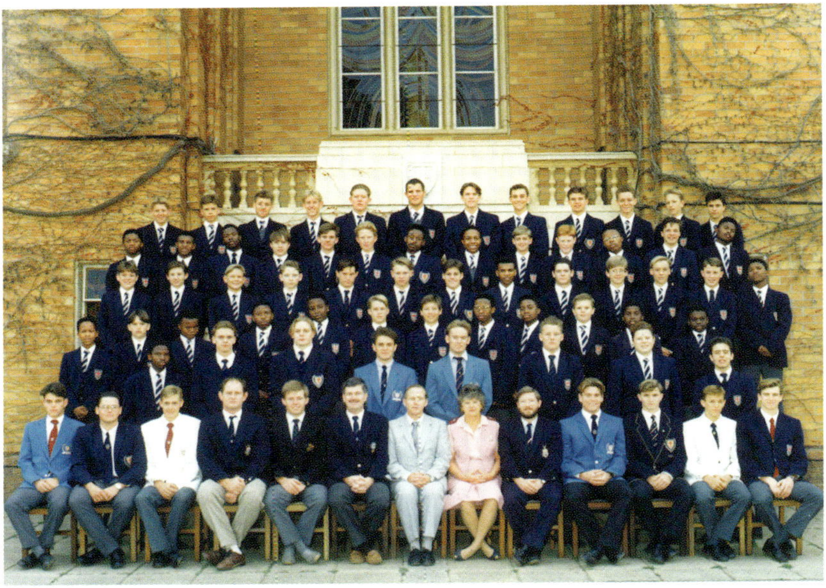

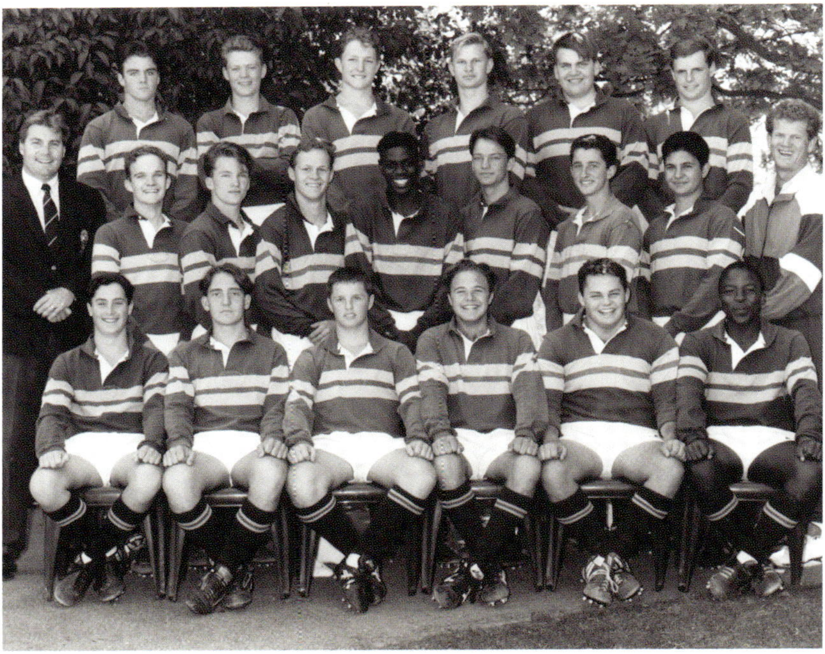

OPPOSITE PAGE

TOP: Kabelo (second row from the bottom, far left) in Mountstephens House at St Stithians College, 1993. (Courtesy of St Stithians College)

BOTTOM: Kabelo (bottom row, far right) in the 2nd XV Rugby Team at St Stithians College, 1994. (Courtesy of St Stithians College)

THIS PAGE

TOP: Kabelo (second row from the bottom, sixth from left) in matric class photo at St Stithians College, 1995. (Courtesy of St Stithians College)

BOTTOM: TKZee, with Tokollo Tshabalala (left), Zwai Bala (centre), and Kabelo (crouching), 1998. (Media24/*Drum* Magazine/Gallo Images)

TOP: Kabelo performing in 2004 in Newtown, Johannesburg, before he started his running and fitness programme. (Sydney Seshibedi/*Sunday Times*)

ABOVE: TKZee performed together for the first time in 10 years at Metro FM's 23rd birthday party in Sebokeng, 2009. (Oupa Bopare/Gallo Images)

RIGHT: Kabelo in 2007, three years into his training regime. (*Drum* Magazine/Gallo Images)

TOP: Kabelo and Danny K are co-founders of ShoutSA, a local music initiative to raise money to fight crime, 2010. (Bongiwe Gumede/Gallo Images)

LEFT: Kabelo taking part in his first Comrades Marathon, 16 June 2006. (Felix Dlangamandla/*Beeld*)

Kabelo with Gail and baby, Zoe.
(Jacqui Whyte)

I actually was never body conscious; when I had a big belly I never looked in the mirror. Even early in 2006, I wasn't checking up on how I looked. But I remember when I started noticing my body. It was at a concert. We were performing – it was a TKZee reunion show, at Mary Fitzgerald Square. I remember taking my shirt off. People were talking, saying how good I was looking. When I saw the picture of me that got published in the newspapers, I was like: wow! From then on, I was *always* topless on stage, always finding an excuse to take my top off. For the first time I had definition on my stomach. I became obsessed with myself, and it hasn't stopped. I went from being fat to being a sex symbol! The girls started noticing ...

The whole time I was training on my own. I ran once or twice with other people but I didn't want to run with anybody else on a regular basis. I loved that time by myself, loved hitting the road. Especially when I started running those 58-minute runs – how my body started moving, how my heart rate started handling. When, before, I was gasping for air, now I was smashing the same course. I was conquering the hills. I definitely knew there was something there.

Before I went to run the race at Akasia, I met another person who would play an important role in turning me into a Comrades runner. I went to Sportsmans Warehouse one day, to get some stuff, and there was a woman called Megan Jaffray, who was selling supplements. I started chatting to her, and she suggested I tried out some of her products. Megan was big into using sports nutrition for performance. She introduced me to goos, electrolytes, endurance shakes. She told me to use a carbohydrate shake when I was going to be running for three hours or more. For shorter distances like 10 kilometres, your body can use what's there – maybe even up to 18 kilometres, depending on how fast you run. But longer than that, and your body needs more sustenance. Many people get stuck, from a performance perspective, because they don't understand the value of the right nutrition *during* performance. Meeting Megan was divine providence – she had all South African products, and I reacted so well to taking them. My Comrades experience would have been nowhere near what it was if I had not had sports nutrition. I still use all of those products when I run. (See the material contained in the section 'Run, Eat, Live: A Guide from 0-89 Kilometres' for an expert guide to running and nutrition.)

The Akasia 3-in-1 – there was a marathon, a half-marathon, and a 10-kilometre route – was the first time I had entered a race. It was also the first time I would be running not just with other people, but with a *lot* of other people. I drove all the way to Pretoria, I got stuck in traffic, I struggled to get parking. Then I had to get my number, had to remember to take my shake, had to remember my music. By that time I had invested in a moonbag, or a running pouch; I was wearing my heavy running shoes – I was only starting to learn about different shoes, and about shoe rotation, which Megan was teaching me – and a string vest, and those really ugly polyester shorts that some runners wear. I was still big. I was very scared. And I was thinking: this is *it*. This was the gauge as to whether or not I would be able to do Comrades. The rule of thumb is, if you can finish a normal marathon in under five hours, you'll be able to complete the Comrades ultramarathon within the cut-off time.

I have pretty much blurred everything from that race. The only image I have of me on that day is me running. I remember going around for the second lap and thinking, oh my God ... Somewhere along the route there were these young girls on the side of the road, chanting, '*Hou bene, hou bene*', and my *bene* needed to *hou* big time.

I knew there was just one hill, and the second time I just smashed it, because it was close to the end. When I hit 36 kilometres, I knew I was on about four hours. I remember reaching the finish, coming around that last corner and seeing the big watch over the finish line, seeing that it said 4h45m. And in my mind I knew it. I knew I could finish Comrades.

The next race that Nick Bester made me run was the Longtom ultramarathon, from Sabie to Lydenburg in Mpumalanga.

By this time Nick was getting a bit more involved with my training. There was a lot of media attention – with this overweight ex-addict attempting Comrades – and his name was attached to it. I think that mattered to him. And, being the performer and the professional that he is, he wanted it to work.

I drove with Nick from Johannesburg to Sabie. On the way in, we got onto what would be the route for the run – only, of course, Nick didn't say this while we were driving. He only told us at the end. He said, don't worry, it's just time on your legs. You only have to worry about one hill. But that hill was 38 kilometres long. 'That route we just drove now,' he said, as we got to the bottom of this hill, 'you guys have to run all the way to the top.'

I stayed in Sabie at like this VIP camp, one with all the top runners ... and me. The other runners, maybe they knew me from my music, but they couldn't put two and two together in terms of thinking that I was actually going to run this race. I had the same questions: what the hell am I doing here? Why am I doing this again?

The other runners, they didn't care really. Top runners just don't get what happens at the other end of the scale. This one time, I was sharing my 10-kilometre time and my marathon time, and they laughed. In my face. It wasn't even a malicious laugh, it was just like: come on, you're messing around. Sipho Ngomane – he had won Comrades the year before – he just didn't get what I was doing there. I was like: if I can just do Comrades in 11 hours ... He was a contender to win the race. But he wasn't unkind; they weren't trying to be harsh.

We went for a run in a nearby forest, to get used to the high altitude. It wasn't a long run, maybe it was two or four kilometres. It was way too short, if you had asked me. At that stage I didn't know what a taper run was. For the top runners, it was a warm-down before the main event. For them it was a trot. Some of the ladies stuck with me for a while. The guys just bolted. I had my music, my headphones. I couldn't have cared less, really. When we were done, we headed back to the camp and I went back to my own room.

You know those little blankets or those teddy bears that kids carry? That was what my music was to me. I'd downloaded Lenny Kravitz onto my iPod. I was focused on the music. I was totally out of my comfort zone, with these runners in this forest in the middle of nowhere. But I was still focused on my mission. I fell back onto all the training I had been putting in. I was the one who had made a big noise about doing the race. And I was doing it for charity. The thought of that kept me going.

What continued to motivate me was my friends, the people I was hanging out with, who continued to be a little bit shocked. 'Dude, are you really going to be able to do this?' they would ask. I kind of liked that. Not necessarily just proving people wrong, but the challenge it implied. I felt alive, like I was doing something.

Also, I was really seeing this 'after drugs' person. At rehab, they had told us about the miracles of recovery. If you follow the suggestions we lay out for you, they said, you will stay clean – and you will discover the 'miracles of recovery'. They didn't say what those miracles were. I was busy wondering, what the hell is a miracle of recovery?

Well, Comrades was one of those miracles. After that, I was hell-bent on discovering more!

On the day of the Longtom race the elites were in their own world. They were pretty unsocial, but that's completely understandable. I had my own supplements with me. I just remember being alone for most of the time. Because I hadn't run Two Oceans earlier that year, Longtom was my ultra – I had seven hours to finish 56 kilometres. It was a *tough* run.

We all headed to the start together – it was my first experience of leaving for a race completely in the dark. When I had run at Akasia, I remembered it being quite a lot lighter. This Longtom, I was in the middle of nature, it was pitch black. Next thing I knew it was time to get up, get my goos, get my music. Sabie was such a quiet town, but that morning it came alive. All of these runners came out of the woodwork. The top guys were with the top guys. I was on my own. I can't remember where Nick was.

It wasn't a big race, in terms of numbers, and that was quite different to what I would experience later, when I ran Comrades, when I ran Two Oceans – then there are always chunks of people around you. This race, I ran with people for maybe the first 10 kilometres or 20 kilometres; after that the field separated.

I never really wanted to run with people when I was training, but at a race, the presence of all these other runners has a completely different dynamic. And it's incredible. You could be running with ... Piet Skiet van Tonder and his wife; you could spend 50 kilometres together; or you could be running with Alf Kumalo. And that's what is amazing about running – this thing where everybody's drama, everybody's history literally gets forgotten, and you just become runners in the same race.

My favourite is when a motorist tries to get through the road marshals, or drives where they're not supposed to be driving, or throws a rude gesture at the runners because they're annoyed at having to wait maybe five minutes. Suddenly there are 2 000 runners ready to take you on. Everybody's got each other's backs.

For those four, five, six, seven hours of a race, we become human again. We let each other be. You can be running with a delivery van driver and the CEO of a big company, and your standing in society, your credentials ... they mean nothing when you have seven hours to run. You feed off each other, keep going. I wish we could replicate that in everyday life. I guess that's maybe why people keep on coming back. The road is one place where all this crap doesn't exist for a couple of hours.

At the beginning of a race I usually don't talk to anyone. I just want to get to the other side. I only start thinking about the noise, the people around me, when the battery on my iPod goes flat, and I only really start smiling and chatting when I know there's just a few kilometres left to go.

The Longtom race was all about distance – what Nick had described as 'time on your legs' – and it was about mental preparation. That year was an 'up' Comrades (from Durban to Pietermaritzburg). The wisdom was that, if you were training for an 'up' Comrades, you should run Longtom. There wasn't any particular pressure on me – I had already qualified for Comrades, I was *in* the race – but it was a test of the will, and a test of my body.

It was quite crisp when the race started. Slowly the sun started to creep up, but it was still quite dark. I remember running in a group of people, crossing a bridge and looking at all the vegetation around me – it was green, there were lots of forests. I was trying to pace myself, and I was marvelling at these guys who, in the first few kilometres, would have fat, *loud* conversations. I just thought of this as energy expenditure – that they were chowing energy they would need later.

Past the 40-kilometre mark was no-man's land – even though I've run 89 kilometres, I still call it that. When I'm training, it's different. Then everything over 21 kilometres is no-man's land. Uncharted territory. But this time it really was unknown ground. I'd never run further than a marathon.

Around that stage I was alone. The cars that picked up the cones had already started driving along the road, and the guys who were cleaning up all the water stations were just slightly behind me. I was kind of with the last of the runners. There was always maybe 30 metres, 40 metres between the guy who was behind me and the guy who was in front of me. It was a very lonely race. I would run-walk-run-walk. At that stage I didn't know how to measure my rate per kilometre, what was six minutes a kilometre.

I remember reaching the top of the Long Tom Pass, which was the highest part of the route. I saw the signs for Lyndeburg, and there was this statue, this old cannon. And when I reached that point I thought, flip. I'm actually nearly there. I'm going to make it. I got a second wind. I put on the Lenny Kravitz album; when 'Fly Away' came on, I just bolted. I had this bounce in my step. I ran, non-stop, from there right to the finish.

When I got to the finish I could see that the party was long over. But I didn't care – I'd made it, in six hours and 48 minutes.

Once I'd crossed the finish line I had to go looking for everyone else; of course, they had finished hours ago. But I was over the moon. I was euphoric. I had run an ultra, I had run 56 kilometres!

From the finish we got into the van and drove straight back to Joburg.

And, then, it was time for Comrades.

Everything and Nothing to Prove

The night before I ran my first Comrades Marathon, there were messages of support pouring in on my phone, everyone telling me they loved me so much. It literally felt like I was going to die the next day. My mom was more restrained. She told me I had nothing to prove, that I was her champion, and that she would still love me whatever happened. I don't get those messages any more now. Except from my mom, of course.

Between the time I finished running Longtom and the start of the Comrades Marathon, there were about eight weeks. I carried on following the programme Nick Bester had given me – he would still send me stuff to do. I was running around 60 kilometres a week – and that was all I had to do, keep running. Everything else was sorted – the flights, accommodation, transport.

I met Bruce Fordyce for the first time when we arrived at the hotel in Durban. It was surreal. I think he was the reason I ran this bloody thing. He gave me such great advice – he said that every single step you take on the day is a step forward. Every single step must be forward. Even if you're talking, keep walking. He also said that the atmosphere on the day itself gives you 30 kilometres in the bag, easy.

It's the rest you have to work for. And it's true – you wake up, and you're almost halfway ...

Even before the race, the atmosphere was incredible. It was amazing for me to see the branding in its setting at the Comrades expo – that iconic image, the person running, that looks a little bit like the Interflora logo. We got to the expo centre early, missed the queues, got our ChampionChips (the computer chips that track each runner's run, which are tied to the runner's shoes during the event). When I was there I carried on doing interview after interview. There was still a strong sense of disbelief – was Kabelo actually going to do this thing? A few days before the race Dave from Reebok had driven the route with me. The whole time during the drive, there was this look of uncertainty on his face, like he wasn't sure I could pull it off. Driving the route totally put me in my place. Just when you thought it was over, there was another 20 kilometres. And then another 10 kilometres. I didn't speak to Dave all the way back to Durban.

When I registered at the race expo I got my number, 34041 – it's still my number today – and I got my H seeding. Now, H is the last seeding, right there at the back. The seeding is based on your qualifying marathon time, so it wasn't really a surprise – but it still freaked me out a little bit. I started wondering what it would mean, in practical terms. The gun going off ... and then you are so far back that you take six or seven minutes to get to the start. They don't take that time into account when they make the cut-offs! I was *kakking* myself, because at the pace that I was running then, I would *just* make it in 11 hours. And if there was no credit for those six or seven minutes, then I might not make it. In the end, I was stressing for nothing. But at the time ... flip!

On the morning of the race I woke up super early, got my goos and my gear ready, made sure I had a carb shake an hour before the start. Dave was going to be seconding me that day, and he took all my stuff with him. He was a Durbanite, he knew all the roads backwards, and I knew I could completely rely on his support. He made me feel confident.

I think I drove to the start with the Harmony Gold elites. But they went to the front of the pack, and then I got dropped off at H.

I knew the time had come when we started singing 'Shosholoza'. There I was: I had made it to the start of Comrades. I was *at* the start of the Comrades Marathon. Then the rooster crows, then the cannon goes. The gun goes 'doef', and we are all still standing still. We started walking, slowly. People were having conversations with each other. Our momentum picked up slowly but surely, and eventually we started running. These days I have a B seeding, but I actually miss starting at the back, starting so slowly and gently.

The race itself was surreal. There had been so much media hype about my participation that, from 10 kilometres in, people who knew that I was running would see me, and they would go bananas, screaming out support for me. It really helped.

There were all these other runners around me – and, you know, mostly no one really knows who anyone is, but the other runners who were with me, they got involved too. At one time, other runners formed a circle around me to block off fans, to stop people from trying to run me down.

At maybe 50 kilometres, there were people standing with banners that read: 'WHERE ARE YOU, KABELO?' And the runners would shout, 'Here's Kabelo!' At 50 kilometres in, that kind of encouragement is exactly what you need.

I could never have made it without all those people, without the massive support all the way along the whole route. I ran past schools; I was cheered by thousands of kids who had listened to my music. I was very spoiled. Those people, they carry you. I literally felt like I had a chaperone. Guys would even get me water – I was really given the VIP treatment.

Of course it also comes down to the running. But you need that support, you welcome people supporting you, and you draw from that energy. After the first three Comrades, it died down a bit.

That first race, the group of runners around me were all chasing 11 hours just like I was. At the start of the race I stuck with the 11 hour bus – those are the pace-setters who help you stick to and reach your set time – but it wasn't my rhythm. Just as I felt I was getting warm he would stop, and then he would start. So I stayed just ahead of the bus, and made friends with another smaller group of runners who had decided to do the same. 'That bus is not catching us,' we said to each other. On the day, those were my best friends.

Dave was an absolutely phenomenal second. When we had driven the route, he had told me where he was going to be, at different stages in the race. But it felt like every time I looked up, he was there shouting for me. And he was exactly where he said he was going to be, exactly when I needed him. Seeing a familiar face throughout the day was like divine providence. Everything worked. Everything was just perfect on that day. I long for that race again. I have had one or two other races like that, but the rest were just proper hard work.

Even through all the cheering and the crowds, running 89 kilometres was still painful. I felt it particularly during the quiet parts; those were the stages I liked the least. There are obviously always pockets of people, but there are still those places where it's a lot more quiet, and where it's really hurting. You can be alert, you can be hydrated, but it still hurts. And you're not the only one who is hurting. Seeing other people fall by the wayside is quite scary. Literally, you see people falling off the road – especially past the 60-kilometre mark. A dream deferred, a dream destroyed. The ambulances, the shuttles, they are so tempting. The driver passes right alongside you, and if you want to stop – and of course you want to stop – you could just stop, and get in the van. But if the guy drives even one metre with you in it, then you're disqualified. And you have to deal with your own hurt and your own doubts, and you also have to deal with watching someone else's dream being shattered right in front of you.

Then you reach Hillcrest, and you're getting closer to halfway, and the crowd picks up again and so does your energy.

At Inchanga – which is one of the five big hills on the race, and the longest hill on the route – that was when it *really* started to get sore for me. My legs were hurting. I was running and walking. My music was all that kept me going. Every now and then I would feel a spike of pressure – a reminder that I was the one who had made a big noise about running Comrades. That receiving the money for charity was solely dependent on me actually finishing the race. It was a good pressure.

The names of all the hills literally got drummed into me before the race – by Dave, and by other people at Reebok.

I finally got to Polly Shortts – the 'one', the dreaded hill, the one that hits you when you've already run almost 80 kilometres but *this hill*, you think, *how the hell am I going to make it?* – and I *ran* up that hill! I figured, if I was running up Polly Shortts, I could smell blood. I was almost there.

The fans in that area recognised me – and they also knew the stadium wasn't too far off. Those people lived around the corner from the stadium, and their cheers were different. Now there were less than 10 kilometres to go, I started feeling a bounce in my step. With six or seven kilometres to go, my music gave me an extra push. The runners around me confirmed that we would all definitely make the 11-hour cut. We even took a break and walked a little.

As the noise of the crowd started to change, we also started seeing that the demarcation on the road was different. This was the final approach to the stadium. That part, for me, was the best. There's a big live camera about three kilometres out, so if they pick you up there they have time to prepare. I had a hit out at that time, 'It's My House', and, as I ran into the stadium, they started playing it. The entire arena erupted. It was like I was performing to this massive crowd; people were on their feet. Nick was there, Bruce was there. The paramedics who were taking care of people ... when they announced on the PA that I was running in, the medics put their stretchers down to see me.

It felt like a hero's welcome. On the other side of the fencing, people all around me were going off their heads. I had made it – in 10 hours and 51 minutes. The way everyone in the stadium reacted, to me it felt like I had won the race. It was over too soon, that moment. I wish I could have bottled it. And it wasn't even recorded! I get upset about that sometimes.

I think the reason that race was so 'perfect' was that I had nothing else to compare it to. There I was, actually running the Comrades Marathon – something my peers in the music industry, the public at large, had all thought was pretty much impossible.

Dave Turnbull also played a large part in that experience. Then, I didn't know the route the way I do now. I literally stepped out in faith. And he was always where he said he was going to be. It just felt great – one of those rare moments when everything was working together.

I've run seven Comrades marathons since then. These days there's a lot less fanfare, and now, I tell myself, now I am *actually* running the Comrades. Without all the fuss and fanfare you get to see what you are really made of. Now I only have my faith in God, and the preparation I've put in, to get me to the other side.

Faith Records

> *Success is in the details. It lies in being reliable, returning emails, showing up on time. I started my own record company off the back of a very successful solo career. That success made me feel like anything was possible – what could be so hard about running a record label? I quickly learned that being in studio was cool, making the music was great, but when it came to going out and promoting music, getting stuff on radio, shooting music videos, managing artists, dealing with infighting ... I wasn't necessarily cut out for it. All the artists I initially signed have since gotten releases and gone on with their careers. But the silver lining is that I got to set up an infrastructure that allowed me to own all my intellectual property as a solo artist. In hindsight, that was the step I needed to take.*

My last platinum-selling album, *Exodus*, came out in 2006. Two years before that, I had started my own record label, Faith Records. It was a natural progression, from being an artist to wanting to own the majority of my intellectual property.

Owning a record label, I learned a few big lessons quite quickly – mostly that the skills you need to be a successful artist were not the same as the ones you need to be a successful record company boss! Suddenly you're dealing with people's careers; you're responsible for people's lives. It takes a lot of the fun out of the job, when it's not just about the music, when it's about administration.

At the same time, I was dealing with my other big dilemma: I was really getting into my faith, and was trying to work out whether I was secular, whether I should be a gospel singer instead, whether I should try and produce more positive music. It affected my creativity. I didn't have a direction. Public perception about me had also changed. I was no longer this kwaito bad boy. Me, the fans, I think we all felt: oy, where do we go from here?

The sound had also started changing – the sound I had played an integral part in creating, that started changing. It left me ... at sixes and sevens. Was I supposed to stay true to where I'd started? Did I need to change with the times? I'd like to think I have always been about progress. The thing that allowed me, and others, to be the architects of the sound we made – to make kwaito – was that we were about progress, about moving forward, about creating new things.

But I still had to come up with the goods as a musician, and I wasn't first off the mark, which meant I was now playing catch-up. It was frustrating. I tried to morph my sound with new sounds, but it didn't catch on. People had moved on. When I released *I'm a King* at the end of 2007, I didn't know whether I was coming or going. I don't know *what* that album was about. As a record label owner, it was all about getting product on the market, about paying expenses to keep the company afloat. But my creativity was in the sewer. Those were the dark, lean years for my creativity.

It was while I was in studio, working on *I'm a King*, that I got involved with Danny K, to set up the SHOUT Foundation. I was busy recording a hip-hop version of' Tears For Fears song, 'Shout'. Danny, I think, was working with the same producer. One day he walked into the studio in a bit of a state – this was after Lucky Dube had been killed, and Danny's parents had also been victims of crime. He said to me, 'We need to do something. We need to speak out against this.'

When he said that to me, my life was already focused on the idea of service. I didn't have to think twice about it. Because I was recording 'Shout', we took that song in another direction, and got tens of other acts into the studio to record the song we used to launch our campaign. It was something that started with a small idea, and mushroomed into this big thing. It felt good, it still feels good, to be a part of something that inspires hope.

I believe everything is divine providence. I was still working, I was being an active citizen. But those lean years were *still* hard. My saving grace was that I had been in the music business for so long, I had built a repertoire that kept me relevant and that still inspired the guys who were now on the come-up. The longevity of my career was, on some level, inspirational. I believe I was a landmark for many artists. That's what kept me alive. But I was forced to start thinking differently. After I hosted the SAMAs one year, I also realised there were other avenues I was interested in pursuing. I've always been very interested in exploiting my brands on different platforms – following my counterparts overseas. I worked with a cellphone company on a mobile phone range, releasing a whole album and a music video on those phones. I tried to look for innovative ways to create different revenue streams.

But, at the end of the day, I'm still a musician through and through. That's when I'm most alive. I still felt I needed traction in the marketplace when it came to my music.

There had been talk of a TKZee reunion for the longest time and in 2009 we got together and released *Coming Home*. We were all game, but recording the album, so many dynamics had changed. I was off drugs. Zwai was married and already had a kid. Before, we were in a very particular space. We were young, we had no inhibitions. Now I was more calculating. I wasn't living paycheque to paycheque; I was thinking: what do the next five years look like? So it was a strange time in studio. The quiet guy who was content to let Tokollo and Zwai take the wheels, he didn't exist any more. Now there were three driven individuals, each of whom knew exactly what he wanted, what he was doing. There were three heads, and anything with more than one head can be a monster. Although the TKZee brand still had equity, by our standards, by commercial standards, the album was a failure. It didn't even sell gold.

I know I was lucky to have a great start in the music business. And I'm hell-bent on leaving a legacy. But it will be on my own terms.

After *Coming Home* I just soldiered on. I decided to release a trilogy – the first volume of *Immortal* came out in 2011, the second in 2013, and the third volume in 2015. The principles I had learned when I first went out as a solo artist still applied. It was all a matter of me humbling myself, picking up the phone, and calling people. I had the confidence that I *could* work with the new-school producers.

During that time Mafikizolo – who had started a few years after TKZee – came back with a monster album. It inspired me to dream again. They were one of the acts that had been around as long as I had. And they not only staged a comeback, they shot the lights out. To me, both Theo and Nhlanhla are a lesson in resilience. Their story has been well-documented. They have soldiered on through it all.

You Have to Forget Past Victories

Compared to Comrades, I see the Two Oceans Ultra Marathon as a very kind race. It allows you to warm up. The small hills come at the right time. Your heart rate spikes and, just as you hit your threshold, you get a downhill. Maybe it's because the route is 30 kilometres shorter than Comrades, but the Two Oceans route is easier for me to remember. And I always find that when you know the route very well, you know how to pace yourself. The first 28 kilometres or so, it's quite busy on the road. You go through the suburbs, it's packed with spectators and families. Then, just before Chapman's Peak, there is this awesome silence. It's exactly the same silence every year. It's the sound of runners' feet running up Chapman's Peak. When I reach that place, that's when the race really starts.

There are different medals for finishing a Comrades Marathon. The first 10 men and 10 women to cross the finish get a gold. After that, every runner who makes it past the finish line in under six hours – that means five hours, 59 minutes and 59 seconds (5h59m59s) – gets a Wally Hayward medal. Those are your elites. From six hours to exactly seven hours, 29 minutes and 59 seconds (7h29m59s), you get a silver medal. After that, there is the Bill Rowan medal, for runners who finish the race in under nine hours (again, that means you have to cross the finish line *before* nine hours, at 8h59m59s), then comes the bronze medals. The old cut-off time for Comrades was 11 hours, and everyone who finishes the race within that time gets a bronze medal. From 11 hours to 11h59m59s, there is now what is known as the Vic Clapham medal. And then there is the final gun, after which there are no more finishers, just heartbreak.

The first year I ran Comrades I finished in 10 hours and 51 minutes. In that kind of race, nine minutes can be a lifetime. In Comrades, even 10 seconds can make all the difference in the world. Nick Bester had always said to me that 11 hours was the original cut-off time for Comrades, and so that was the time I needed to make. I listened to Nick.

The following year was a 'down' run – Pietermaritzburg to Durban – which was a different proposition altogether. I was so pumped for the race. You're running down for the majority of the run, which sounds like it should be faster – but it requires a completely different energy, a different muscle system. I actually ran slower. That year I finished Comrades in 10 hours and 54 minutes. But I wanted to do better. I still had Nick Bester helping me with training. I was always meeting these top Harmony Gold runners who Nick was associated with. The elite runners mostly intimidated me, but they also inspired me.

There's really only one kind of runner that guys like Nick Bester recognise – and that is that lean, elite runner, the one who can run 10 kilometres in under 30 minutes. I was quite big for a runner, even though I had lost a lot of weight by then. But Nick still gave me his time, and I will always be grateful for that investment. I always felt like I had stuff to aim for. And so my next goal was to finish Comrades in under 10 hours.

I adjusted my training accordingly. I was still doing all my running on my own; I carried on running the same distances but I guess, the natural order of things kicked in: my weight continued to come down. Over the years I got lighter and fitter, and I got faster. There really wasn't that big a difference, for me, running it in under 11 hours and doing the same thing in less than 10. What did change, though, was that my marathon time started improving. By 2008 I was running marathons at around six minutes a kilometre, and I finished a marathon in four hours and 12 minutes. I thought that if I could run 42 kilometres in that time, I could definitely finish Comrades in under 10 hours – because Comrades is like two marathons, and some change. To run a sub-10-hour Comrades, I needed to reach halfway in five hours. And if you come in for your first half at four hours and 50–55 minutes, you're on your way – and then the other half kind of sorts itself out, especially on an up run. My marathon time showed me that I could easily achieve that. That year, I managed to finish the race in nine hours, 59 minutes. I think that may have also been the year I spoke to Tim Noakes, who told me to walk as much as I could during the first half – after that, the second half would sort itself. You walk the distance between one lamppost and the next, then you run to the next lamppost. Then I started getting braver: I would walk for two lampposts, and run for two.

The next year I managed to do my first sub-nine-hour Comrades. That meant a different medal, and different training. That year I remember spinning a lot. The speed work on the bicycle in class helped with my fast-twitch muscles; it programmed my body to move very quickly. I also started getting more into my sports nutrition with

Megan, looking at taking carbohydrates and electrolytes during the race, replenishing what the body was burning and losing, and doing more body conditioning. Megan made me do kettlebell training with her! My marathon time started to come down even further – I was finishing a marathon in under four hours; I did a three-hour, 51-minute marathon, and was running at around five minutes, 30 seconds a kilometre. With that speed, there was no ways I was running a 10-hour Comrades. I worked out that all I needed to do to get in under nine hours was to come in halfway at around four and a half hours. That was the method I used, the sum total of my 'strategy'. I think I also got my time down because I carried on losing weight, and my strength-to-body-weight ratio had changed. At my first Comrades I probably weighed about 90 kilograms. By the time I ran Comrades in eight hours and 46 minutes, I was nearly 10 kilograms lighter.

When I ran my fifth Comrades Marathon I got my time down to eight hours and 23 minutes. I started including more marathons in my race preparation – I would run the Soweto Marathon, the Pick n Pay Marathon, do the Two Oceans Ultra Marathon. In my regular training, I added a 28-kilometre course around my house. I wasn't working with Nick any more; I was kind of just doing it by myself. I knew the time I needed to be running, and I just went ahead and did it. To be honest, I was just addicted to the endorphins, how it made me feel. When the endorphins would really kick in was when I would start to motor.

On my sixth Comrades, I ran a much slower time – back up to eight hours and 46 minutes, which I wasn't very happy about. I had run Two Oceans just a few weeks before, and I had finished the ultramarathon in four hours and 28 minutes. That was on a Saturday. Then, two days later, on the Monday, I climbed on a plane and flew to Australia, and drove 300 kilometres to go and climb Mount Kosciuszko, the highest mountain there. I was on this mission to climb the seven highest peaks in the world – later that year I would attempt Aconcagua in Argentina, but I only made it to 6 200 metres when bad conditions forced us to bail. I was doing this with the mountaineer Alex Harris, and we were both training for different things. So once we'd climbed to the top of Mount Kosciuszko, we agreed that we would *run* back down – which we did! Then we went to sleep, woke up, got into the car, drove 300 kilometres back to the airport, and flew back to South Africa. And then a couple of weeks later I ran Comrades. I thought I would smash it – but I was too tired. Comrades had other plans for me. By the time I was approaching Pietermaritzburg I was just finished. That said, even when things 'fell apart' for me at Comrades, I was still determined that I was not going to go over nine hours!

The following year I didn't run. This has become kind of a pattern with me: I get the performance shock of my life, and the next year I don't run Comrades. In 2012, on the day of the Comrades Marathon, I had a concert with TKZee in Kenya. But that year I met a running coach. I started working on a new programme. My marathon time came down again – now I was coming in at under three and a half hours. I hit my best time at the Soweto Marathon: I clocked three hours and 27 minutes. I was over the moon. Knowing that I could challenge that kind of marathon time put me into a different league in running circles. You're not anywhere close to the elites, but three hours and 30 minutes is good running. You're not brilliant, but you definitely don't suck. You start to see yourself as a proper athlete – not world-class maybe, but intermediate.

In 2013 I ran Comrades in eight hours and 13 minutes. The next year I decided I was going to go for a silver medal – that meant I had to finish the race in under seven and a half hours.

Although I had already shaved almost three hours off my Comrades time, from when I started running, the closer I got to my threshold the harder it was to cross.

I went back to a dietitian (see the 'Nutrition' section for our expert's eating plan), I had an amazing coach. We started doing track work to increase my splits – which made sense: if I was faster on the track, I would be faster on the road. My aim was to get my 10-kilometre time to under 40 minutes, and get my marathon time to under three hours. The best I managed was finishing 10 kilometres in 43 minutes, and then I did a marathon in three hours and seven minutes. I came 42nd in that race – the Secunda 3-in-1 – it was unbelievable. I came into the stadium, and there were still single runners coming in!

I was flying on the track; I was flying on the road. It was my year for silver. By the time I got to the Comrades expo I felt full of confidence. But it still hadn't quite settled into my mind, that it was achievable. I knew Comrades was one of those races – where nothing is a given. It was, in one way, when I was going from 10 hours to nine hours. There, mathematically, it made sense. But now my halfway split meant there was a lot more pressure. If I was going to make Comrades in under seven hours and 30 minutes, I had to reach halfway within three hours and 45 minutes. My best marathon time was three hours and seven minutes; that meant I only had a 38-minute leeway – which seemed like it was still a lot, but I was worried it wouldn't be enough. There was also the issue of pace. I needed to run at a pace of five minutes per kilometre. The *whole* way. When I made my marathon time of three hours and seven minutes, that was a really flat race – there were no hills. And Comrades has more than just a few hills to deal with!

I also wasn't fully listening to my trainer, in terms of taking time to rest. I didn't listen to my body. I would do a 13-kilometre run because that was what was on the programme, even though I still hadn't recovered from my session the day before. That was a real lesson for me – one I am trying to pay attention to now. If your body is not ready for the fifth run of the week, sit it out. Don't just tick off 100 kilometres and focus on mileage, mileage, mileage, because that's what it says on a piece of paper. Listen to your body. A good day out is a good day out. Take it in and appreciate it for what it is. But you also have to build up to those good days – and they can't all be good days. I was trying to have these perfect 45-minute/10-kilometre runs three times a week. The discipline of rest has been one of the hardest things for me to learn. And what happens to me when I do take time off? I come back stronger the next day!

Ten Minutes Too Early

My mother always thinks I push myself too hard. The night before Comrades, she'll tell me to relax, to have fun. It helps to remember that it is fun, and not to take things too seriously. These days I'm the person sending scary text messages to other people – especially the ones I know are doing Comrades for the first time – telling them to be very afraid, that it will be the hardest day of their life. That's what Nick and everyone did to me! That fear actually helped a lot in my first race. You have to go in there not disrespecting it at all, have the utmost respect for Comrades without having run even one step. If you go in respecting Comrades, then you stand a chance.

When I got to the start of the 2014 Comrades Marathon I was nervous. We went through all the usual rituals: singing 'Shosholoza', the cock crowing, the cannon, and then we were off. You usually know, within the first five kilometres, whether or not you're going to have a good race. I was gasping for breath; I could feel what was like a build-up of lactic acid in my muscles, although I wasn't sure if it *was* lactic acid, or if I just needed to warm up properly. And all the time, my mind only had one thought, on repeat: *I need to run five minutes a kilometre. I need to run five minutes a kilometre.* This was counter to my own advice, and it worked against me.

Because I needed to be as light as possible to contend for silver, it was the first time I had run the race without having all my stuff on me – I had left everything with my running club. This was an added stress for me, wondering where they would be. Sometimes their stand would be as much as four kilometres out from where I had expected them. This wasn't their fault – it's about what the route allows – but it was difficult.

By the time I was 18 kilometres in I could feel I just didn't have enough *oomph* – usually this was when I would have started to feel good; 15 kilometres is generally the magic mark for me, when it all starts to kick in, and I can feel the carb shake starting to work, and my muscles are warm. I carried on running. Sometimes the body just needs a bit longer to kick in. But the day ahead started looking longer and less certain. I had to start making my time goals, and I was worried. Before halfway, I knew I would hit the monster hill at Inchanga – and on the down section I could make up a lot of time. But that's all I was doing. I was constantly making up time, constantly catching up.

At the halfway mark – I had meant to come in at around three hours, 45 minutes – I came in 10 minutes early, which was already a bad sign. On one level, the time pepped me up; it made me think that maybe I did have what it took to get a silver. I handled it for about five kilometres after the halfway mark, and then the wheels started to come off. I started walking. And, last time I checked, I don't think it's possible to do a Comrades Marathon in under seven and a half hours if you walk some of the parts.

It was those extra 10 minutes that made me think I could walk for a bit on the other side of the halfway mark. But if you've already used up that energy, it's gone. You can't get it back by walking. It's always better to conserve what you have than to try and rest to get back what you've already consumed. As cool as it seems to have extra time 'in the bag', those 10 minutes meant that I had actually gone too fast. And by then, my legs were really starting to feel it. I got a slight second wind in Hillcrest – it's a nice suburb, and the streets were packed with supporters, which always spurs me on a bit. My wife was waiting there, with friends of ours. When you see your wife, you can *only* be honest. It's like having a mirror. She will ask you how you feel, and it's her – who are you trying to kid? While I was running, I saw her, and I stopped. I stopped running and I walked to her. Even from five, 10 metres away, she said she could see that I was stuffed. And I still had 33 kilometres to go.

At that stage I think I had given up on the silver dream. It had disappeared somewhere between the halfway mark and Hillcrest. I knew it wasn't going to happen for me. Now it was just a matter of survival. That's how Comrades is; you can go from trying to clock a Personal Best to not finishing at all. But I was still intent on carrying on, and I was still committed to finishing the race in under nine hours. But, like I said, Comrades is such a strange race. After Hillcrest came Botha's Hill; running down that hill, I was in so much pain. I thought I still had a carb shake to take, that maybe that would give me the energy I was missing. But my running club weren't where they were supposed to be.

As it turned out, the boost I needed wasn't a shake or a goo. I carried on running, looking for my club, and I met this other guy I knew – one of the people I considered to be a top runner. He would always wear these compression socks, and so you could see him from a mile away. His race had also fallen apart. We saw each other, we were probably wondering, about the other guy, what the hell happened here? I was thinking, flip, if even *this guy* has lost it, then I'm in even deeper trouble than I thought.

We started hobbling along together. We ran two or three kilometres, and by then the pain was excruciating. Somewhere along the way we met another guy. It was his first Comrades. He asked if he could run with us. And, just like that, the three of us committed to sticking together until the finish line. When they needed to stop or take a leak, I stopped for them. When I was ready to quit, those guys would tell me to get up and keep going, you're almost there.

My body was telling me that I was done. I was ready to start walking. I was close enough that, even if I did that, I would still make the finish in under 12 hours. But those guys wouldn't let me. They said they would walk with me for as long as I wanted to walk – but that we would all finish together. I think I would have got into one of those shuttles if it wasn't for them.

So we literally plodded along; we would run for 50 steps, then stop and walk. Sometimes, if we felt a bit better, we would run to the top of the next hill. We got each other through what felt like a very dark period, from 20 kilometres away to 13 kilometres before the end. So much can happen in those seven kilometres, but those guys were there for every step. People were running past us, but we didn't care. We would take turns getting each other water at the water stations. I would see people who I knew were slower than me go past us, and it didn't matter.

By the time we were 13 kilometres out from the finish, we could smell Durban. The crowds started to build up. When we saw this, we said to each other: at least we're going to make it – and we're still getting in at under nine hours! Even in the last two kilometres, we were still walking. We said that when we got to the final kilometre we would run, all the way to the stadium. At that point the crowds also started to recognise me; they started shouting my name, and that helped a lot – every little bit helped. And then we were running into the stadium together, finishing the race together. And I was so grateful for those guys as we crossed the finish. We did it in eight hours and 43 minutes.

When you reach your goals at Comrades, you don't feel the pain so much. You fly up the stairs afterwards. After this race, I knew I was stuffed because I couldn't even walk. It hurts more when you don't get what you were aiming for. All the races before Comrades, you can't afford to feel any hurt, because you know you have to get over it and carry on training. But with Comrades, it's the end of everything – the end of all the training, the big build-up. You don't have to pick yourself up again and go running on Monday. After this, you are off for two or three months. After I finished that race, I don't even know where the other two guys went. I just found myself a corner; I was drinking energy drinks, drinking fizzy drinks, eating, trying to get stuff into my body. People wanted to talk to me but I ignored them. I was just *gatvol*. I know that for most people eight hours, 43 minutes is still a really good time. How many people dream of getting a Bill Rowan medal? I've got five. That puts me in the top 1 000 to 1 500 – out of 20 000 runners! But because I was so focused on the silver, I couldn't see that.

Eventually I made my way to the nice suite that my running club had, where I would meet up with my wife. There were these two guys there – they looked like they hadn't even been for a run – with silver medals around their necks. They looked so happy. One had finished in seven hours and 12 minutes, the other in seven hours and 29 minutes. They were over the moon they'd reached their goal. I was jealous; I was inspired. It's hard to express the feeling.

My wife said: you ran, you finished, well done. But for me, the quest for a silver medal is still on.

I've done a lot of thinking, about why I fail ... people say success is in the details. Maybe I had over-simplified my approach? Once you cross over into silver-medal territory – that seven-hour, 30-minute mark – the game changes completely, and your ability to focus on the details becomes that much more important. The rules that apply when you're in Grade 7 are not going to apply to you when you're in matric.

For Comrades I'd been doing enough effort to get ... a B. I'd been getting a B. But that extra effort, the effort required to get an A? That's ... oy! And that is where I find myself.

In 2014 I honestly thought a silver medal was in the bag. I'd got a coach, I'd done track work. I'd run a marathon in under three hours and 10 minutes. It wasn't the conventional wisdom, that I was fast enough for a silver at Comrades, but it was still possible. After the race, I started to think maybe it wasn't possible. That maybe I had reached my threshold. And then I watched Caroline Wöstmann win the Comrades Marathon, and she inspired me to get back on the road. Two or three years ago, she wasn't on anybody's radar. And she came along and blew everyone away. But she hadn't come out of nowhere: she'd been doing the hard yards, quietly. If you put in the hard yards, if you do the work, you will get the results. It inspired me to get my act together, to improve my diet, to stay focused.

I've Got to be that Guy

For three years before I met my wife, Gail, I was single by choice. I was reading books by Christine Caine, who ministers to a lot of young adults. Her writing reminded me that being single was okay, and that being single was not the same as being alone. When I finally understood that, I decided to stop dating for a while. This allowed me to get to know who I was and what I wanted – and, also, to know what I didn't want. By the time I met Gail, I knew that it was the qualities within rather than the qualities outside a person that mattered. The first time we met, Gail came to one of the home cells I was hosting. It had been ... engineered by a mututal friend, but she didn't even know she was there to meet me. She had just come from work and wasn't dolled up at all. In Matthew it says, 'out of the abundance of the heart, the mouth speaks' – that you are able to tell a person's character by the words they speak. When it was Gail's turn to speak, when she opened her mouth, I knew here was substance. And I knew that, if I was going to be the man I wanted to be, this was the kind of woman I needed to be with. Within a month or two of meeting her, I remember calling my mom and telling her: 'Mom, please get the uncles ready to go.'

I've had countless people come up to me and say they have been inspired by my story. That they are running because I was running. These two worlds – running and entertainment – are usually so far apart, and the music industry comes with so many connotations. I broke the mould. I did something that not many people can do. And, I think, people saw that if this oke could come from there and do that, then maybe they could too.

And you can, you know. You can do it.

I still want to chase silver; and I'd also like to complete an Ironman in under 12 hours. These are my two medium- to long-term goals, and they are important for me. And it's important because, when you are physically fit, your threshold for everything else goes up a notch or two. Your mindset is different. When you're working towards a goal it keeps you in check; it keeps you focused, fit, knowing you are working towards something. I always say, take care of yourself and all your other aspirations become so much easier because you're in the right state of mind. I know that where I am at, physically, influences my attitude and enhances everything.

Endurance is a muscle that needs to be exercised. And you will need this endurance for everything in life. For 90% of the time you don't get what you want, when you want it. They say making it in the music industry is all about nine nos and one yes. You've got to be able to endure those nine nos.

This book comes at a time when ... I'm speaking from hindsight. And it's important for me to document what's gone on in my life. This new season in my life is going to need its own book.

Fatherhood and marriage have meant I've embraced responsibility. Embraced being accountable. And I want to be real about it. For the first time in my life I am actually living and feeling.

When you get married, your wife is like a mirror of who you are. Every time I walk into our home and I stand in front of Gail, I see me. I see my flaws and my strengths. I can't hide anywhere. Only through that mirror of marriage will I be able to see whether I'm making progress as a person.

And if Gail is like a three-dimensional mirror, then our daughter is 4-D, high-definition! She's not even saying a word yet; she just looks at me. But just through her being there, I feel like I am being asked all these questions: what are you doing with your life? What are you doing about your dreams? What are you doing about all the unspoken promises you have made to me? I hear these questions every time I look at her. Answering them is all about action. Getting off my arse, doing what I need to do.

Run, Eat, Live:
A Guide from 0–89 Kilometres

With Ross Tucker, Lindsey Parry and Sarah Chantler

I have told you my running story. And I hope that, in some small way, it has inspired you to want to start running – or to challenge yourself to run further than you once thought you could. But what worked for me might not work for you. I'm only an expert in 'Kabelo running'!

With very few exceptions, anyone can become a runner. How you get there – how fast, how long, how hard you run – is up to you. There is no 'one way' or 'right way' to run, except that you need to keep putting one foot in front of the other. You can do it on your own, like I did; you can do it by running with friends or joining a running club; you can even do it on a treadmill at your gym.

In the pages that follow, you will find training and running programmes designed by two leading sports experts – Ross Tucker, who is professor of exercise physiology at the University of the Free State; and biokineticist Lindsey Parry, who is the official coach of the Comrades Marathon Association and the technical director of the Tuks Athletics Club and Tuks Junior Athletics Academy.

Together with their training programmes, Ross and Lindsey have shared their advice and strategies on how you can be the best (and safest and healthiest) runner you can be. While you may have passed the 10-kilometre mark years ago, or may not plan on ever running a Comrades Marathon, it is still really worth reading all these sections to get their expert insight.

Finally, dietitian Sarah Chantler shares her suggestions and guidelines for healthy eating and hydration, and how to eat/drink as a runner – both during training and on race days. Again, diet and nutrition are very varied and individual, but Sarah's recommendations provide an excellent foundation for creating and maintaining a diet that is both effective and intuitive, rather than prescriptive.

All of these sections are designed to address a wide range of runners – whether you're looking to run just for fun, to finish a race within a cut-off time, or hoping to push your Personal Best into sub-elite territory.

I hope you enjoy the journey.

– *Kabelo*

The Start Line
Ross Tucker

Ross Tucker is professor of exercise physiology with the School of Medicine at the University of the Free State.

One of the biggest barriers to starting anything successfully is that we're often ill-prepared before we start. In an ideal world, before we decided to make the transition to becoming runners we would all be physically active and walking considerable distances every day. But that's not realistic. Most of us spend a large proportion of our time desk-bound, sitting on a chair in front of a computer. And no one wants to start a running programme that says it will take two years before you can run 10 kilometres.

The good news is that, if you're realistic, sensible, and cautious, you can still go from non-runner to 10-kilometre runner in as little as 12 weeks. Excluding people with certain medical conditions (see below), this is less about physical fitness and more about being systematic. The same guidelines for novice runners also apply to more experienced runners wanting to run half-marathons, marathons and even ultramarathons.

Start slow
The main reason people fail is because they start too quickly – they ask too much of themselves in the first few weeks, and then either

get injured or, mentally and physically, find they are not enjoying it.

Be realistic
Some people can run for 20 minutes the first time they get on the road. Some people can't. The key here is to assess your *own* abilities and be realistic. Then you need to rig the game so that you can win it. This means setting up targets for yourself that are achievable. The shortest path to failure is failure. If you set a goal to run five kilometres on your first day out, but you're huffing and puffing by the time you get to the first corner, within a few minutes of starting your ambitious running plan you have already made yourself feel like you are not capable. Rather set smaller goals and achieve them. Once you start conquering your goals, then it's time to be more aggressive.

My experience is that women are much more likely to underestimate what they're capable of. Men are more likely to overestimate themselves. This means a woman may take 12 weeks to reach 10 kilometres – when she could have maybe done it in eight weeks. A man may get to the same distance in six weeks and may get injured.

Expect structural weaknesses
It's important to remember that training is a stress, and that you are *looking* for stress, asking your body to adapt to it, and become fitter. The other reason people start and then stop running is because it exposes structural 'weaknesses' in your body – things you never knew about when you were sitting in front of a computer. Running will bring out little things in your knees, your feet, your hips ... The best way to deal with this is, first, to be cautious and conservative (see

above) and, also, to do your running in parallel with another exercise routine that focuses on the lower back, trunk and core muscles in particular. Pilates is a good example.

It's important to understand that you almost certainly *are* going to have some niggles. Adaptation is not a silent thing. Delayed-onset muscle soreness the day after a run is one symptom of adaptation. Your body is repairing 'damage' in a way that will make muscles stronger and more resilient; you'll end up better off than you were before, but the process of getting there is painful. Your foot might get sore under the arch; your Achilles tendon might flare up; your shins, knees and hips might complain.

These are not necessarily signs to stop – but they are signs to pull back just a little, maybe cut your workout by 20%. For example, if you're doing a 25-minute session, drop it down to 20 minutes. If the pain persists go down to 15 minutes. In most instances, that reduction will take care of the niggle. If you ignore it and keep on pushing, keep on increasing your training time, that's when a niggle can become a serious problem. Rather swallow your pride and lose a few minutes, than have to take off two or three weeks of injury time.

If the shoe's comfortable, wear it

There are hundreds of studies and articles devoted to running shoes – and which ones are best (or worst) for you. The consensus at the moment is surprisingly simple: the main thing is that the shoe you wear must be comfortable. And, if it's comfortable from the very first time you wear it, you're least likely to injure. So, if you're buying your first pair of running shoes, forget the fancy gels and devices, just put the shoe on, walk (and run) around, and whichever shoes feel most comfortable, go for that pair.

Go for time + exertion, rather than distance or pace
The running programmes and strategies included in this book focus on using time as a guide to get you up to the required distance. This allows you to run at your own pace – the pace your body is okay with. It's also easier to measure minutes, and doesn't require any fancy tracking devices or gadgets.

The second factor to take into account, together with time, is 'perceived exertion' – essentially how hard you're pushing yourself, relative to yourself. So if one represents no exertion or effort at all, and 10 is an almost impossible maximum effort, you would want to aim for an exertion somewhere around five, increasing to six, at most a seven (imagining that eight, for example, would be where you started breathing heavily or were having difficulty breathing easily). Calibrating the numbers in between one and 10 comes from listening to your own body. (There is also a more detailed Borg RPE [Rating of Perceived Exertion] scale, which runs from six to 20, and can easily be found online.)

The idea is to mix time and exertion, so you improve a *tiny* bit at a time. You want to finish each session feeling like you've conquered it – and that you could have done 'one more': one more kilometre, one more repetition, one more minute. Never finish feeling like you've burned out the match completely.

Medical conditions
Certain people *should* have a medical (a consultation with a doctor or specialist, to get medical clearance) before they start any new exercise programme. This includes people with risk factors for cardiovascular disease (CVD) – such as a family history of CVD or heart attacks, high cholesterol, diabetes, and high blood pressure. If

you have had prior CVD events, or any other chronic health condition where running might not be indicated, it's best to work with your doctor(s), and take your first steps under their supervision.

Be aware of your self
As you progress through your running programme, you will gradually become more self-aware as a runner – and this will allow you to be guided by your own body, and your own perceptions, rather than any formula. One of the tools you can use to become a more discerning, self-aware runner is to write it down: keep a daily journal, log book, or even an Excel spreadsheet that notes how many minutes you ran, what your overall perception was of the run, and if you experienced any niggles. As your distance increases, you will also want to add information about your hydration, nutrition, and even the shoes or clothing you wear.

Ross Tucker's 12-Week, 10-Kilometre Programme

This is a programme designed for novice runners. Each week is broken down into three sessions – ideally these should not be done consecutively, but with a non-running or rest day in between. As your running fitness improves, you can start introducing consecutive running days.

The bracket after each exercise indicates the number of times the described set must be repeated within one session.

WEEK 1

1) 1-minute run + 3-minute walk (5)
2) 1-minute run + 2-minute walk (6)
3) 2-minute run + 2-minute walk (4)

WEEK 2

1) 2-minute run + 2-minute walk (5)
2) 3-minute run + 2-minute walk (5)
3) 3-minute run + 2-minute walk (5)

WEEK 3

1) 4-minute run + 2-minute walk (4)
2) 4-minute run + 2-minute walk (5)

3) 5-minute run + 2-minute walk (4)

WEEK 4
1) 5-minute run + 2-minute walk (4)
2) 6-minute run + 2-minute walk (4)
3) 5-minute run + 2-minute walk (5)

WEEK 5
1) 5-minute run + 2-minute walk (5)
2) 6-minute run + 2-minute walk (5)
3) 6-minute run + 2-minute walk (5)

WEEK 6
1) 6-minute run + 2-minute walk (5)
2) 7-minute run + 2-minute walk (4)
3) 6-minute run + 2-minute walk (6)

WEEK 7
1) 8-minute run + 2-minute walk (4)
2) 8-minute run + 2-minute walk (4)
3) 9-minute run + 2-minute walk (4)

WEEK 8
1) 12-minute run + 2-minute walk (3)
2) 9-minute run + 2-minute walk (4)
3) 10-minute run + 2-minute walk (4)

WEEK 9

1) 20-minute run + 2-minute walk + 15-minute run (1)
2) 10-minute run + 2-minute walk (4)
3) 15-minute run + 2-minute walk (2)

WEEK 10

1) 20-minute run + 2-minute walk (2)
2) 10-minute run + 2-minute walk (5)
3) 15-minute run + 2-minute walk + 10-minute run + 2-minute walk + 10-minute run (1)

WEEK 11

1) 15-minute run + 2-minute walk (3)
2) 25-minute run + 2-minute walk + 15-minute run + 2-minute walk + 5-minute run (1)
3) 30-minute run (1)

WEEK 12

1) 30-minute run + 2-minute walk (2)
2) 30-minute run + 2-minute walk + 15-minute run + 2-minute walk + 10-minute run (1)
3) 25-minute run + 2-minute walk (2)

Running a Half-Marathon
Ross Tucker

Generally someone who can run 10 kilometres will be able to finish 21.1 kilometres without massive alterations to their training – simply by adding in one longer run per week (see programme on the following pages). The key here, again, is to focus on time not pace. If you get hung-up on pace it's a recipe for over-training. Go and run for 90 minutes. It doesn't matter if you run it at six minutes or six minutes and 30 seconds per kilometre – just get the time on your feet.

Get it right

Increasing 'time on your feet', or time on the road, means a slightly higher chance of niggles or injury – simply because the risk of injury is proportional to the dose of running – but the type of injury is no different, and still affects the same places: the plantar fascia (the ligament or connective tissue that runs under the arch of your foot, connecting your heel bone to your toes), Achilles tendon, knee, calf, shin ... As you become a more experienced and self-aware runner, you will, hopefully, be able to work out what can be resolved through rest and training management (cutting back your programme, as with the previous section), through self-treatment, and what requires a professional consultation, for example with a physiotherapist. At this stage of your running, nutrition may also start to play a more important role – both during the race (see the 'Nutrition' section that follows further on in this book), and in terms of your general health. People who are under-nourished are more likely to get immune suppressed and get ill during training.

Setting different goals?

If you're setting time goals instead of distance goals (let's say you've already managed a half-marathon – or even a longer distance – and are now looking to improve your finishing time) the secret is to break down your running into stages, almost as you would have done at the start, and reverse-engineer the race with your new goals in mind.

To play with pace, always focus on the under-distance – you'll get your 10-kilometre time down by focusing on your five-kilometre pace, etc – and go for speed first, before bringing the distance back up. Depending on your goal, you may want to break it down even further, to single kilometres. Don't try running eight kilometres at four minutes and 50 seconds a kay – rather do one kilometre at that pace, with a three-minute jog in between, and repeat it several times, so you gradually teach your body what it feels like. The more advanced you become as a runner, the more your training goes back to how novices train: run, walk. The reason for this is you want to teach your body about Frequency, Intensity and Time (FIT) – these are the three variables in a training session. And you only want to increase one or two in any given session (that is, trying to jump up your frequency, intensity *and* total time all at once is a recipe for either failing or injuring yourself). If you're increasing any one of these factors, you'll also need to increase your rest time.

Ross Tucker's Nine-Week, Half-Marathon Programme

These programmes assume a reasonable current level of running fitness (see the previous programme for 10 kilometres), and are not recommended for runners starting from scratch. For novice runners, first complete the 10-kilometre programme.

The intensity of this nine-week programme varies depending on your own current level of running fitness. For this programme, runners are broken down as follows:

A: Runners who have run the half-marathon distance before, in a time between 1h45 and 2h00, and who are currently running three times a week (1h45 programme).

B: Runners who have run the half-marathon distance before, in a time between 2h00 and 2h15, or a 10-kilometre in 55 to 60 minutes (2h00 programme).

C: First-time half-marathoners, or those who currently run 10 kilometres in between 65 and 70 minutes or more, and who want to finish the Two Oceans Half-marathon comfortably in under three hours (2h30 to 3h00 programme).

- All programmes include a weekly five-kilometre Park Run (or, from Week 3, a local 10-kilometre race) on Saturdays. Formal races and Park Runs are a great way to get used to running with people, and help you push harder while simultaneously managing your effort. For runners working at the A and B pace, these runs teach your body how to handle heightened intensity without working at your maximum pace. A and B runners should include an 'easy' 20- to 25-minute warm-up or an easy pace for the first 10 to 15 minutes of the five-kilometre run (or 15 to 25 minutes of your 10-kilometre race); C runners should allow for a 10- to 15-minute warm-up before the five-kilometre run. As fitness progresses, the five-kilometre and 10-kilometre runs should be done at race tempo.

- Every second week, hill or interval sessions will be introduced to increase your strength and stamina. Here you should challenge yourself.
- For C runners, the run/walk strategy reduces the risk of injury, and should be part of your strategy on the actual race day – plan to walk before you have to walk!

Numbers in brackets indicate the number of times the exercise should be repeated. Your weekly long runs should be done slower than your actual race pace.

The following pace/exertion terms are used:
- 'Very fast' = five-kilometre race pace
- 'Fast' = running at 10-kilometre race pace
- 'Easy' = six to seven out of 10 on your own perceived exertion scale
- 'Harder' = eight out of 10
- 'Comfortable' = five out of 10

Week 1	A (1h45)	B (2h00)	C (2h30)
Monday	40 minutes easy	Rest	Rest
Tuesday	35 minutes easy	35 minutes easy	10 minutes easy / two minutes walk (3)
Wednesday	Rest	Rest	Rest
Thursday	25 minutes easy / 25 minutes harder	25 minutes easy / 25 minutes harder	10 minutes easy / two minutes walk (3)
Friday	Rest	Rest	Rest
Saturday	Park Run	Park Run	Park Run
Sunday	60 minutes easy	Rest	Rest

Week 2	A (1h45)	B (2h00)	C (2h30)
Monday	Rest	Rest	Rest
Tuesday	Intervals • Five minutes warm-up • Six minutes fast run / four minutes slow jog (4) • Five minutes easy to finish	Intervals • Five minutes warm-up • Six minutes fast run / four minutes very slow jog (3) • Five minutes easy to finish	15 minutes run / two minutes walk – comfortable (3)
Wednesday	45 minutes easy	Rest	Rest
Thursday	50 minutes very easy	40 minutes easy	20 minutes run / two minutes walk (2)
Friday	Rest	Rest	Rest
Saturday	Park Run	Park Run	Park Run
Sunday	1h20 easy run	60 minutes easy (include walks)	20-minute run / two-minute walk (3)

Week 3	A (1h45)	B (2h00)	C (2h30)
Monday	Rest	Rest	Rest
Tuesday	35 minutes easy	35 minutes easy	20-minute run / two-minute walk (2)
Wednesday	Hill session • 10 minutes easy to warm-up • Three minutes hard uphill (5) – slow jog downhill • 10 minutes easy recovery to end	Hill session • 10 minutes easy to warm-up • Three minutes hard uphill (5) – slow jog downhill • 10 minutes easy recovery to end	Hill session • Five minutes easy to warm-up • Three minutes uphill / walk down recovery (5) • Five minutes easy recovery to end
Thursday	35 minutes easy	Rest	Rest
Friday	Rest	Rest	Rest
Saturday	Five-kilometre Park Run or 10-kilometre race	Five-kilometre Park Run or 10-kilometre race	Five-kilometre Park Run
Sunday	1h30 easy (include hills in second half)	1h20 easy (include hills in second half)	20-minute run / two-minute walk (4)

Week 4	A (1h45)	B (2h00)	C (2h30)
Monday	Rest	Rest	Rest
Tuesday	40 minutes easy	40 minutes easy	20-minute run / two-minute walk (2)
Wednesday	Intervals • Five-minute warm-up • Six-minute fast run / four-minute slow jog (5) • Five minutes easy to finish	Intervals • Five-minute warm-up • Six-minute fast run / four-minute slow jog (5) • Five minutes easy to finish	Rest
Thursday	35 minutes easy (slower than normal)	Rest	30 minutes easy
Friday	30 minutes very easy	30 minutes easy	Rest
Saturday	Five-kilometre Park Run	Five-kilometre Park Run	Five-kilometre Park Run
Sunday	1h45 run (include hills in second half)	1h40 run (include hills in second half)	30-minute run / three-minute walk (3)

I RAN FOR MY LIFE

Week 5	A (1h45)	B (2h00)	C (2h30)
Monday	Rest	Rest	Rest
Tuesday	45-minute run on hilly route; push uphill, easy downhill	45-minute run on hilly route; push uphill, easy downhill	35-minute easy
Wednesday	35-minute easy	35-minute easy	Rest
Thursday	Rest	30-minute easy	Hill session • Five-minute easy to warm-up • Three-minute uphill / walk down recovery (6) • Five-minute easy recovery to end
Friday	40 minutes easy	Rest	Rest
Saturday	Five-kilometre Park Run or 10-kilometre race	Five-kilometre Park Run or 10-kilometre race	Five-kilometre Park Run
Sunday	1h10 run	1h10 run	20-minute run / two-minute walk (3)

Week 6	A (1h45)	B (2h00)	C (2h30)
Monday	Rest	Rest	Rest
Tuesday	35 minutes very easy	35 minutes very easy	35 minutes very easy
Wednesday	Hill session • 15 minutes easy to warm-up • Three minutes hard uphill (5) – slow jog downhill • 10 minutes easy recovery to end	Hill session • 15 minutes easy to warm-up • Three minutes hard uphill (5) – slow jog downhill • 10 minutes easy recovery to end	20-minute run / two-minute walk (2)
Thursday	45 minutes easy	45 minutes easy	10-minute run / two-minute walk (3)
Friday	Rest	Rest	Rest
Saturday	Five-kilometre Park Run	Five-kilometre Park Run	Five-kilometre Park Run
Sunday	1h50-minute run	1h50-minute run	10-minute run / two-minute walk (8)

KABELO MABALANE

Week 7	A (1h45)	B (2h00)	C (2h30)
Monday	Rest	Rest	Rest
Tuesday	Rest	Rest	40 minutes very easy
Wednesday	Intervals • Five-minute warm-up • Three minutes very fast run / three minutes very slow jog (6) • Five minutes easy to finish	Intervals • Five-minute warm-up • Three minutes very fast run / three minutes very slow jog (6) • Five minutes easy to finish	Rest
Thursday	45 minutes easy	45 minutes easy	Intervals • Five-minute warm-up • Three minutes very fast run / three minutes very slow jog (6) • Five minutes easy to finish
Friday	Rest	Rest	Rest
Saturday	Five-kilometre Park Run	Five-kilometre Park Run	Five-kilometre Park Run
Sunday	1h20 run	1h20 run	15-minute run / three-minute walk (7)

Week 8	A (1h45)	B (2h00)	C (2h30)
Monday	Rest	Rest	Rest
Tuesday	60-minute easy	60-minute easy	50-minute easy
Wednesday	Intervals • Five-minute warm-up • Three-minute very fast run / three-minute very slow jog (8) • Five minutes easy to finish	Intervals • Five-minute warm-up • Three-minute very fast run / three-minute very slow jog (8) • Five minutes easy to finish	20-minute run / two-minute walk (2)
Thursday	45 minutes easy	45 minutes easy	35 minutes easy
Friday	Rest	Rest	Rest

Saturday	45 minutes easy	45 minutes easy	Five-kilometre Park Run
Sunday	50 minutes easy	50 minutes easy	60 minutes easy

Week 9	A (1h45)	B (2h00)	C (2h30)
Monday	Rest	Rest	Rest
Tuesday	45 minutes easy run – finish with five fast runs of 150 metres each, with a slow walk back in between to recover	45 minutes easy run – finish with five fast runs of 150 metres each, with a slow walk back in between to recover	20-minute run / two-minute walk (2)
Wednesday	20 minutes very easy	20 minutes very easy	20 minutes very easy
Thursday	Rest	Rest	Rest
Friday	Five-kilometre very easy run in the morning – finish with five 150-metre runs at race tempo	Five-kilometre very easy run in the morning – finish with five 150-metre runs at race tempo	Five-kilometre very easy run in the morning – finish with five 150-metre runs at race tempo
Saturday	RACE	RACE	RACE
Sunday	Rest	Rest	Rest

Marathons and Ultramarathons
Ross Tucker

This section covers programmes for both marathons and ultramarathons, up to 56 kilometres (the Two Oceans Ultra), and can also be used as a foundation for Comrades Marathon training. For specific additional Comrades Marathon training and race strategies, see the next section.

The shift from 21.1 kilometres to a full marathon, and even an ultramarathon, is less than you think – and more than you think. It's not that you need to train differently; it's just that you need to train more. And the more time you spend on your feet and on the road, the more there is that can go wrong. Once your distance increases, your margin for error becomes much smaller. In order to get a marathon done a lot needs to go right, and you can't afford for much to go wrong. Missing a session, or missing a week (due to work, travel, illness or injury) starts to become a lot more significant than it did when you were running 10 kilometres or 21 kilometres. If a busy work schedule means you can only train once or twice, what used to be 'no big deal' potentially becomes a big setback. More time on your feet also means that the risk of injury becomes higher and, because you're running more (more often, and for longer periods), there are far fewer opportunities to recover.

Training for a marathon means you will have to make some

lifestyle sacrifices (and your family might have to make some too) – more runs, and more long runs, mean less time for socialising, less family time ... While many individuals over-emphasise the mileage you need to put in, you will need to find the balance between training *enough* (taking lifestyle/family sacrifices into account, together with your personal running goals) and training *too much*. You may be able to do a marathon running 60 kilometres a week – but you'll run a better one if you're putting in 70 kilometres ... although the latter will squeeze your non-running time, and allow fewer days off, fewer short runs and less time for recovery. At this stage, how you eat, how you sleep and what you do in between, starts to become really important.

Cross-train
Elite runners spend between 90 minutes and two hours a day doing some form of core-focused cross-training, such as Pilates – it's fundamental to their running. For non-elite runners, this doesn't mean you have to spend an hour a day in a Pilates studio (although if you have the time, then great!). Even if you have half-a-dozen Pilates or similar exercises you can do at home (like exercises while sitting on a Pilates ball), these will improve your running. This is *particularly* important if you're sitting at a desk for most of the day: you can't run a strong marathon if you're a desk jockey for eight hours a day and a runner for one. Activities such as spinning, swimming and cycling can also help maintain your fitness, or give you a 'break' from running while effectively keeping your training going. It's never a bad idea, every five or six weeks, to run less and swim or bike more, if you have that option.

Strength doesn't mean bulking up

What you *do* want to avoid is doing any form of strength training that will build up excess muscle bulk. Long-distance runners are generally not built like Mr Universe – the magic happens in the tendons, not the muscles. Being bulky on the road is a non-functional strength, and is not only unnecessary but also means you are carrying additional weight (which you don't want). You need a different kind of strength for running. Your knees, Achilles ... they are connected to your muscles, and the stability of those joints is heavily influenced by how stable your muscles are. So you don't necessarily need to be 'strong', but you need to develop the strength-endurance of the muscle.

If you're going to train in a gym, be careful about how much weight you lift, how often, and what kind of lifting you do. For most people, resistance exercises using body weight alone is enough – calf raises, squats and lunges are enough for the kind of strength a runner needs. If you want a formal programme, speak to someone who can put exercises together in the right way for your running needs – either a biokineticist or a personal trainer who has a track record with runners (rather than a trainer who is focused on making you big and strong).

Finally, you need to prioritise sleep – and get as much sleep as you can, without it becoming a luxury (and, if possible, take the luxury).

Ross Tucker's 10-Week Marathon and Ultramarathon Programme

This programme is designed for distances from 42.2 kilometres (a marathon) up to 56 kilometres (a Two Oceans Ultra Marathon), and can also be used as a foundation programme for runners training to run the Comrades Marathon. This is not a programme for novice runners, but should only be started by runners who have already completed both 10- and 21-kilometre distances and who are reasonably running fit.

Training notes: As with 10 kilometres/21 kilometres, the baseline running requirements for either a 42- or 56-kilometre (or even 89-kilometre) run are very similar – except that, while a long training run for a marathon runner would be between 30 kilometres and 34 kilometres, for an ultra runner the marathon becomes the long run (and, for Comrades runners, an ultra like the Two Oceans Ultra Marathon becomes your stepping stone). For those looking to run an ultramarathon, a marathon qualifier is built into the programme in Week 5.

The idea with this programme is, through systematic and consistent effort, not only to maintain and gradually improve your running fitness, but also, on your weekly long runs, to give you a chance to try out the diet and hydration strategies, and to plan your walking, as you would for your Big Race.

For all runners – whether you're looking to run a marathon in under three hours and 30 minutes, to finish the Two Oceans Ultra Marathon within six hours, or just to make the Comrades in less than 12 hours – this programme emphasises time rather than only distance, and exertion rather than a specific pace. This means that, even when the training item is the same, it is possible to individualise between and even within each training group (so, what's an 'easy' pace for someone in the A group will be very different for someone running in the D group – and that's okay!). Note that weekends must include one long run (either on Saturday or Sunday), with the other day as a rest day. The final week of the programme includes a rest-taper strategy.

The training 'bands' for this programme are as follows:
A: 3h30 to 4h00 marathon time / five-hour ultra (56 kilometres).
B: 4h00 to 4h15 marathon time / six-hour ultra (56 kilometres).
C: 4h15 to 4h40 marathon time / six-and-a-half-hour ultra (56 kilometres).
D: 4h40 marathon or slower (or novice) / seven-hour ultra (56 kilometres).

WEEK 1:

Monday: 14 kilometres hilly route – hard on uphill, easy on descent (all groups)

Tuesday: Easy eight kilometres (all groups)

Wednesday: Club Time Trial (TT) *or* tempo session: two-kilometre easy warm-up, six kilometres hard, two-kilometre easy warm-down (all groups)

Thursday: Easy 10 kilometres (all groups)

Friday: Rest (everyone)
Saturday/Sunday: 3h00 long run – 30 kilometres easy (A+B) / 24 kilometres easy (C+D). Rest on the other day.

WEEK 2:

Monday: 10 kilometres hilly route – steady tempo uphill and downhill (all groups)
Tuesday: Rest (all groups)
Wednesday: Easy nine kilometres (all groups)
Thursday: 11 kilometres easy (A+B) / rest (C+D)
Friday: Nine kilometres easy (all groups)
Saturday/Sunday: 3h30 run – 34 kilometres easy (A+B) / 28 kilometres easy (C+D). Rest on the other day.

WEEK 3:

Monday: 12 kilometres hilly route – steady uphill, easy downhill (all groups)
Tuesday: Easy eight kilometres (all groups)
Wednesday: Hill session – 300 metres gradual incline: fast / hard up, slow run down to recover (eight repeats) (all groups)
Thursday: Rest (all groups)
Friday: Easy eight kilometres (all groups)
Saturday/Sunday: 3h30 long run – 36 kilometres (A+B) / 32 kilometres (C+D) *note the faster pace from the week before.* Rest on the other day.

WEEK 4:

Monday: Rest to allow recovery from long run (all groups)
Tuesday: Tempo run – five-minute warm-up / 30-minute steady

(half-marathon pace) / five-minute recovery jog / 20-minute fast (10-kilometre race pace) / 10-minute easy finish (all groups)

Wednesday: Easy eight kilometres (A+B) / rest (C+D)

Thursday: Easy eight kilometres (all groups)

Friday: Rest (all groups)

Saturday/Sunday: Medium run at marathon target pace – 22 kilometres (A+B) / 18 kilometres (C+D). Rest on the other day.

WEEK 5:

Monday: Two-kilometre easy warm-up, 10-kilometre steady run (half-marathon pace) (all groups)

Tuesday: Rest (all groups)

Wednesday: Club TT (eight kilometres or five kilometres) – not faster than marathon pace (all groups)

Thursday: Very easy eight kilometres (all groups)

Friday: Very easy five kilometres in the morning (all groups)

Saturday/Sunday: Marathon qualifier (all groups, if needed) or long run – 35 kilometres (A+B) / 25 kilometres (C+D). Rest on the other day.

WEEK 6:

Monday: Rest (all groups)

Tuesday: Route including hills – push on the uphills, very easy on downhills, 90 minutes (A) / 60 minutes (B+C) / 50 minutes (D)

Wednesday: Club TT with 15-minute warm-up and 10-minute warm-down *or* tempo session: two kilometres easy warm-up, six kilometres hard, two kilometres easy warm-down (A+B+C). For D runners: 15 minutes easy / 25 minutes steady (half-marathon pace) / 15 minutes easy finish.

Thursday: Easy 11 kilometres (A) / easy nine kilometres (B+C) / 45 minutes very easy (D)

Friday: Rest (all groups)

Saturday/Sunday: Long run – pace and time depending on group:

A – 4h30 (slower than race pace)

B+C – 3h30 (slower than race pace)

D – 4h00 (slower than race pace; mix running and walking)

Rest on the other day

WEEK 7:

Monday: Rest (all groups)

Tuesday: Rest (A) / 45 minutes very easy (B+C+D)

Wednesday: 90 minutes very easy (A) / 45 minutes very easy (B+C+D)

Thursday: 50 minutes easy (A) / tempo run: 15 minutes easy warm-up / 45 minutes half-marathon pace / 10 minutes easy finish (B+C+D)

Friday: Tempo run: 15 minutes easy warm-up / 60 minutes half-marathon pace / 10 minutes easy finish (A) / Rest (B+C+D)

Saturday/Sunday:

A – 60 minutes very easy run

B+C – 40 minutes very easy run

D – 2h00 easy run, slightly faster than race pace

WEEK 8:

Monday:

A – Rest

B+C – 12 kilometres hilly route, steady uphill and slower recovery downhill

D – 60 minutes hilly route, steady uphill and slower recovery downhill

Tuesday:

A – 12 kilometres hilly route, steady uphill and slower recovery downhill

B+C+D – Rest

Wednesday:

A+B+C – Club TT with 15-minute warm-up and 10-minute warm-down *or* tempo session: two kilometres easy warm-up, six kilometres hard, two kilometres easy warm-down

D – Club TT with easy 20-minute run before and very easy 10-minute run after

Thursday:

A+B+C – Rest

D – Very easy 45-minute run

Friday: 50 minutes very easy (A) / 45 minutes very easy (B+C) / 40 minutes very easy (D)

Saturday/Sunday: 90 minutes easy run with hills (don't push too hard uphill). Rest on the other day (all groups).

WEEK 9:

Monday: Rest (A) / 35 minutes very easy (B+C+D)

Tuesday:

A – 12 kilometres very easy

B+C – Speed session: 15 minutes easy warm-up / five repeats of six minutes fast (10-kilometre pace) + four minutes slow jog / 10 minutes easy to finish

D – Tempo run: 15 minutes easy / 45 minutes at half-marathon pace / 10 minutes easy to finish

Wednesday:

A – Tempo run: five-minute warm-up / 30 minutes steady (half-marathon pace) / five-minute recovery jog / 20 minutes fast (10-kilometre pace) / 10 minutes easy finish

B+C+D – 45 minutes very easy

Thursday: Rest (all groups)

Friday: Rest (all groups)

Saturday/Sunday: 70 minutes easy (not faster than race pace) (all groups)

WEEK 10 (RACE WEEK/TAPER PROGRAMME):

Monday: Rest (all groups)

Tuesday: Rest (A) / easy 40 minutes (B+C+D)

Wednesday: Very easy 40 minutes (in the morning if possible; all groups)

Thursday: Very easy 30 minutes (A) / rest (B+C+D)

Friday: Very easy 30 minutes (in the morning if possible; all groups)

Saturday: Race Day

How to Run the Comrades Marathon
Lindsey Parry

Lindsey Parry is a qualified biokineticist and the technical director of the Tuks Athletics Club and Tuks Junior Athletics Academy. He is the official coach of the Comrades Marathon Association.

This section looks at strategies and concepts that will help runners to prepare, physically and mentally, before running a Comrades Marathon, together with strategies for managing the actual race day itself. A complete 'Comrades Finishers' training programme is available on the Comrades Marathon website (www.comrades.com – click on the 'Training' section).

Lindsey also hosts a podcast 'Ask Coach Parry', where he answers specific questions about running and triathlon training. You can find more on Twitter (@AskCoachParry) or Facebook (www.facebook.com/comradescoach)

Before your race
Preparing to run 89 kilometres requires that you do exactly the same things you would do to run 50 kilometres (like Om Die Dam) or 56 kilometres (Two Oceans). After completing a training ultramarathon, the key is not to get carried away with your mileage, not to heap on loads of longer kilometres. Finishing 50 kilometres or more will already have prepared you for going longer.

Enough running vs too much running
Five days a week: Athletes who run in the middle to the back of the pack – those aiming to finish in between 10 and a half and 11 hours – should not be running more than five days a week. Ideally, they should only be running four days a week. This allows recovery to take place. When it is supplemented with non-impact cross-training (see below), you can still make progress in terms of fitness.

Don't overdo the long run: 10-and-a-half-hour to 11-hour runners should complete between 40 kilometres and 60 kilometres a week, including a weekly long run that is not more than 25 kilometres or three hours. Once a month, add in a longer run of 36 to 40 kilometres. If you complete two marathons and one ultramarathon in the three to four months before Comrades, then you have spent enough time on your legs. People place too much importance on long runs, and don't give enough credit to the sum of their training.

Don't try squeeze everything in: Faster runners, from the middle of the pack to around B seeding, should run five times a week and do more specific training (see below). But even sub-elites need at least one day a week of not doing *any* kind of exercise. You need time for physical and mental recovery. Most people work full-time, and they need a day when they are not trying to squeeze everything in.

Strength training and cross-training for Comrades
Whether it's an up or a down race, the Comrades hills can be scary, whichever way you're running them. Most of the damage and pain in the last third of the race is from long downhills, not uphills. This is why it's also essential for runners to do appropriate strength training,

focusing on quads, glutes, and core (all-round). In the Comrades, your quads take the most damage, and your glutes play an important role in stability – so supplementary training should focus on these areas. Exercises like squats, single-leg squats, and step-ups will help.

Most runners (particularly those looking to finish the race in 10 hours or more) will also find that they get better at running by supplementing their programme with cross-training rather than running more – adding non-impact exercises such as spinning, cycling and rowing.

If you're not used to working out at a gym, find a personal trainer with experience in sports to show you how to do exercises properly. If this is not an option, then a standard circuit in a gym will also be good enough.

Speed + strength add-on: Hill training
Faster runners – those from the middle of the pack towards B seeding (finishing between 8 and a half hours and 10 hours) – will benefit from added hill training. This will help with tackling the monster hills, and also make you stronger. Hill work is a pretty safe way for runners to do speed work, because, uphill, it's hard to run fast so you injure yourself. People tend to overdo speed work on the track, and fartleks. Hill work is safer, and should be done on its own, plus used as preparation for any track work.

For sub-elite runners, two-minute hill repeats are long enough to give you a really good workout – just long enough so your legs start to burn, but not so long that you experience problems in your Achilles, calves or glutes. Work on time (two minutes) rather than distance.

Depending on the level of the runner, start with between three and five repetitions each week (that is, two-minute hill work, repeated three to five times), adding an extra repetition as you progress. For slower runners, max out at eight repetitions; faster runners max out at ten to twelve repetitions.

Keep it simple. Repeat
There are many coaches who create rather complicated workout schedules, with lots of variety. While this may keep the athlete stimulated and interested, it doesn't easily allow for real progress, or measurement of progress. Doing similar things on similar days, over a long period of time, is the best way to improve.

Niggles and injuries
The more experienced you become as a runner, the better you will be able to figure out what will get better simply by running it out, what needs rest, and what needs to be dealt with more carefully. In the beginning (when you start running, or start a new programme to increase your distance or pace), *any* unusual pain or soreness (even stiffness) is a sign you should stop and rest for a day or two. If you take time to recover, your body will come back stronger.

For local injuries, apply ice two to three times a day, and take at least one day of complete rest – no running, cycling, or anything. From the second day on, if you're pain-free it's fine to resume training.

Most injuries or niggles *will* clear up in 24 to 48 hours. If they don't, it's probably time to see your physiotherapist or doctor.

Managing Your Race

Forget 'time in the bag'

Over the past decade, I have been trying to teach runners that their pace should be slightly slower in the first half of the Comrades, and slightly faster (or even) in the second half of the race. But the idea of 'time in the bag' is such a tradition that it's proved very difficult to shift. The truth is, most athletes that I coach tend to run faster in the second half, and that is because they are running the race at an appropriate speed. Most *finishers* run at least 40 minutes slower in the second half.

Because there is this resistance to a negative split, I recommend planning your pacing chart accordingly.

In a 'down' run, the hardest kilometres are the first 18 kilometres or so, with a few more testers between 18 kilometres and 50 kilometres. From 50 kilometres to the end, it's mostly downhill. If you have saved yourself for the end game and are just able to run, you're going to run much faster!

Catching the bus vs missing the bus

Pacing charts – you can find these in running magazines, download them from the internet, or get them from your running club – are a *guide* to the pace at which you hope to run your Comrades Marathon. But the most important thing is how you feel on the day. If your chart says you need to be running at five minutes, 45 seconds a kilometre, but it's not a cruise for you, the reality is you probably won't finish in under nine hours anyway. By insisting on sticking to a pace, rather than going by what your body is telling you, you actually risk not finishing.

Your first two kilometres to 10 kilometres are the most important
The first 10 kilometres are where a lot of people make critical mistakes, mostly due to panic. It can take so much time to cross the start line – particularly if you're at the back of the pack – that you immediately start worrying about making the cut-off. You think: *I lost eight minutes, I'm one kilometre behind schedule* ... But you need to plan for that. Whether you lose 30 seconds or eight minutes, it should be part of your plan before you even get to the race.

Your most important kilometres are the first two kilometres where you are actually running – after you've passed the start line, and after you are able to start moving. These are the only kilometres I really want people to check. This is often when full-blown panic kicks in, and when you start being able to run at the pace you are supposed to be running. You need to make sure the first and second kilometres are at the right pace, not 15 seconds or 20 seconds faster than you're supposed to be running.

For every minute you go through the first half too quickly, you will lose up to four minutes in the second half.

Nothing new on race day!
This is the most basic, and important, advice: do *nothing new on race day*. Whatever your plan is for nutrition, hydration, pacing, walking ... make sure you have tried it out before, at other ultramarathons like Om Die Dam or the Two Oceans Marathon, or on your long runs. You need to know, before the race starts, what works for you, how much fluid you need, that your gels won't make you nauseous ... Look on websites to find out what you can expect to find at the tables along the route.

Keep notes

I tell people to make lists during training – like homework. And the Comrades Marathon is your final exam. As with the previous running programmes, you should keep a journal of your runs (how long you ran for, how far, and how you felt), together with what you ate or drank during the run. Add to this: the shoes you wore, the socks you wore, the vest or shorts or tights you wore; where you chafed or sweated; if you got sunburned on your arms or face or legs ... Use these things to make your list of what you need for Comrades.

When you pack your bag before the race, have that list at hand. This means you will have *everything* you need, and you will know when and where you will be using each item. Keep it with you all the way to Durban or Pietermaritzburg. Of course, some things you won't keep or carry with you – like Vaseline. Find out what is, and isn't, available along the route.

This stuff is less important for silver medallists upwards, because they are not on the road as long, and tend to be more experienced and know themselves better as runners.

The same advice – *nothing new on the day* – applies to your nutrition. Whatever you eat or drink on race day must be something you have tried before. Gels are generally very similar; some have more or less sugar, more or less salt, protein ... The most important thing is their taste, their texture and whether or not you can stomach it (and for how long). I generally recommend gels and sweet stuff in the earlier part of the race, then moving away to savoury, saltier snacks like potatoes, chips, bananas, cheddar squares (again, you must have tried these before on your preceding runs). This sweet-savoury split should, from a performance point of view, be the other way around, but as you run, the blood moves away from your stomach and it becomes harder to deal with a massive hit of glucose, which is why gels can make people feel nauseous later in the race.

Prepare for the race to get tough
As part of your race plan, you need to prepare yourself mentally for when the race gets tough. Even people who have improved their running time, through training, who expect the race to get easier because they are now fitter and stronger, get surprised when they start hurting at the same place as the first time they ran the race.

You need to prepare for the fact that you *are* going to be sore on race day.

Training runs can induce a similar state of discomfort, but because it's usually not that far to go until the end, you are able to maintain your pace without too much difficulty. That knowledge now has to keep you going over Comrades: knowing that, even when you are sore, you *can* keep on going at that pace.

When you reach this part of the race, remind yourself of the work you have done to get to where you are. Repeat your training mantras to yourself – even write them on your arm to keep yourself motivated.

My father, who was a gold medallist, once told me that if you are only sore for the last 20 kilometres of the race, then you've had a good Comrades!

Overcoming failure
Every year there are more than 1 800 runners who do not finish. We generally try to keep this number under 10% of total runners, but in the last few years this figure has been slightly higher.

Failing to finish the Comrades can bring a loss of confidence, and a fear of future failure. Some people respond by not training properly the next year – or by training too much; both will produce the same unsuccessful result. The best thing to do, after a DNF (Did Not Finish) result, is to sit with someone objective, either another experienced runner in your club, or a coach, and try to figure out specifically what went wrong in your race.

A lot of people are scared to approach a coach because they think coaches are only for fast runners – or that, if you approach a coach, you're obliged to stick with them for the entire training programme. But this is not the case. Most coaches will charge you only for a consultation, and will be able to run through many possible scenarios with you.

Run-walk

Run-walk is a powerful physical saving of the body. For a lot of people, it's impossible to run as slowly as they need to run in order to do this. So walking is gold. It changes the muscle contractions, reduces impact and allows you to rest on the move. As with your pace, dress, nutrition, walking is something you must have done before during your training runs building up to Comrades. Don't try anything new on race day.

For the middle to back-of-the-pack runners, try and walk one minute for every 10 minutes you run. For those runners going at a Bill Rowan (sub-nine-hour pace), walk at least one to two minutes for every five kilometres to 10 kilometres. For those going for a silver medal (under seven hours, 30 minutes), walk for one minute out of every 10 kilometres, with extra walks on the big climbs. Be open to doing extra walk breaks on the long hard climbs.

A good strategy to try out on your local or training races is to mix running and walking on a steep climb: walk a little in the first third of the climb; run the middle third; then walk a little again in the last third. During the second walking stretch, you'll often find that you are walking uphill the same speed as or faster than those around you are running. Slower paced runners can try running for one pole, walking for one pole, while tackling steep climbs.

After the race

I am a firm believer in taking at least three weeks' rest after finishing the Comrades Marathon. The first week (probably the first two weeks) should be complete rest, physical and mental. Take time to plug back into your family life, or your social life. If you're smart, you'll couple the rest period with a holiday together with your family. If you've pushed hard at the training races before Comrades – like Two Oceans – you should also take some time off after that.

Nutrition
Sarah Chantler

Sarah Chantler is a registered dietitian at Shelly Meltzer and Associates, the dietary practice associated with the Sports Science Institute of South Africa.

This section does not attempt to provide specific or set eating and meal plans, but looks at best-practice guidelines that will complement and maximise your training and running (including on race days and during recovery) while maintaining your overall health. These guidelines are appropriate for both novice and experienced runners.

The complexity of eating simply

The philosophy of healthy eating 'outside of training' should not vary greatly between runners and non-runners. However, for both the novice and the elite runner, the increase in *energy* requirements to do with running does create additional needs that have to be taken into account. The timing, quantity and quality of the food choices runners make around their training will also have an impact on the way the body optimises its adaptations to training.

While individual requirements and preferences can vary quite dramatically, our national nutritional guidelines do include a surprisingly wide variation of what is considered both 'normal' and 'healthy'. The guidelines recommend more carbohydrate-rich foods relative to protein and fat-dominant foods and include a range for the three macronutrients. The guidelines also encourage caution towards refined sugars and alcohol, and promote fresh fruit and vegetables. Ultimately, the core of every healthy eating programme is similar: it should focus on quality and variety, with an emphasis on fresh and unprocessed ingredients. Keeping the focus on nutrient-rich food (for example, choosing wholegrain bread vs white rolls; grilled chicken breast vs chicken viennas or fresh vegetable vs instant vegetable soup) and ensuring a positive eating environment, will assist runners in creating a healthy intake that works for them.

The reality is that a simple approach (it does not have to be boring!) to how you eat is much more likely to yield long-term and sustainable benefits, both to your overall health, and to your fitness and prowess as an athlete. Just as the running programmes in this book encourage runners to learn to listen to their own bodies, healthy eating involves developing the same kind of *listening* intuition: your body will soon tell you what food works, and what food does not work for you – keeping in mind also that what works for you may not work for someone else, and vice versa.

Some of us may forget how to listen to our bodies. This can include your normal cues of hunger or satiety. We tend to put our nutritional intake at the bottom of the priority list compared to work, family, training etc. Therefore, sometimes we need to take time and put energy into looking at what we are actually eating, and how this should change with training. It is important to be aware that thirst is generally well-regulated, but appetite is not always in direct proportion to our training loads, and needs 'external guidance'.

Keep a food journal
If you are trying to improve your diet, or if you are interested in how your diet is changing as your running increases, you can keep a record by using simple tools such as a mobile phone application, taking photos of your meals, or even through writing/keeping a food journal. This record can be a useful tool in helping you understand what, how and when you really eat, what foods do and don't work for you while you run, and when you experienced any digestive problems during your training. Once you start introducing running-specific products or supplements, like gels, or even sports drinks, you will also need to track how these affect you. Another good starting exercise (pun intended) is to look at what you consider healthy food intake to be – the quality, quantity, food choices, food groups, colours, textures and tastes. Formulating your 'ideal' diet, and then comparing it to what you actually eat, will help reflect on how far you may or may not be from that ideal diet.

Start slow
Just as you wouldn't set off to run 40 kilometres on your first day of running, changing your eating habits is something that needs to be done slowly, and incrementally, in order for you to succeed.

If an eating style works for you, stick to it
We are all unique, and an eating pattern that works for you may not work the same for someone else. If your eating approach has worked for you so far, it is probably not necessary for you to make *dramatic* shifts to your intake. However, if you are aware of problem areas in your day – for example, work functions, late-night snacking, skipping breakfast – you can look at introducing changes in these areas

first. As your training progresses, the focus will need to shift to be more specific to your needs *around your training* in spite of how healthy your approach was to begin with. This will include a focus on the quantity and the quality that you will need to benefit your training load.

Be realistic
Many runners start a running programme with two main goals: to get fit or to lose weight. Specifically for those who have a weight-loss goal in mind, you need to consider your body composition goals in relation to your running or exercise programme, your previous weight-loss experience, your social schedule, family commitments, budget, etc. These factors need to be taken into account in order to help you create *realistic* goals and timeframes. Give yourself a range of weight that you can maintain, rather than trying to keep to a specific weight. If you set yourself unreasonable goals – both from a weight-loss or a performance perspective, like cutting your calorie (kilojoule) content in half overnight, or never eating sweets ever again – you make it almost impossible to succeed. You will either fail on your own, or your eating plan will come crumbling down the first time you have to attend a social event where you are surrounded by enticing finger food. If you like chocolate, it should be included in your ideal eating plan. The amount, frequency and quality are then easier to adjust. The 'trick' to coming up with a plan that actually works is to try find a balance between how you currently eat, and what you *like* to eat, and to work these into your 'ideal' eating plans.

Plan your menu
Training schedules are planned well in advance, so the same principle

should apply to nutrition. Plan an easy weekly menu with options that you enjoy and encourage greater consistency in your eating and nutritional intake around training.

Consistency

Overall, you also need to make changes that you can keep long term, and not sway between an 'on-diet'/'off-diet' scenario where you limit your intake and then over-do it later.

If you are aiming to maintain your current body weight, your intake should match your output. This is another area where many new runners (and even experienced ones) occasionally stumble. Most of us can eat normally, without any additional nutritional intake, and run for 60 to 90 minutes. An hour-long run, sadly, does not equate to the body needing four muffins! However, as your running time and intensity increases, you will need to increase your intake accordingly. In the same way, when your activity decreases – say, when you are resting after a big race, or taking time off – your intake will need to decrease. Otherwise you will experience unnecessary weight gain.

If you are looking for more specific guidelines, the Australian Sports Institute (www.ausport.gov.au) has several excellent factsheets and guides for sports nutrition, nutrition for performance, as well as ones on weight loss.

Extreme eating

Athletes are often tempted to try new extreme ideas to enhance performance or to reduce body weight. To many people, it is a profound disappointment that there is no instant and magic formula that makes you run faster and further, or become thinner (or even richer). This is why fad diets or extreme eating ideas hold such appeal. These diets promise what 'normal' eating does not, and they usually guarantee 'results' within a very short amount of time. Some fad diets in fact do produce quick results, particularly in terms of weight loss. Generally the downside is that, typically, neither the extreme eating regimen nor the weight loss (which often is just water loss) is sustainable. Many fad diets also actively encourage eating behaviours that in the long term can have negative health consequences, including detrimental effects on performance.

Medical conditions
Certain people *should* see a registered dietitian. For example, if you have any chronic lifestyle diseases (including diabetes or cardiovascular disease), have had surgery on your digestive system, have any type of digestive system dysfunction (IBS, IBD), cancer, renal disease, allergies, or are pregnant/breastfeeding or have other concerns where you feel you can't tolerate or include certain foods that might form part of a normal running diet, it will be useful to consult with a registered dietitian who has a special interest in sport nutrition. A dietitian can assist you in creating an ideal plan that takes all your goals, lifestyle and disease concerns into consideration.

Training

Eat to run (don't run to eat)
If you start on a running programme as a novice, and are running three to four times a week for 20 to 30 minutes at a time, you will generally not require anything extra from a nutritional perspective. Once you are doing +/- 10-kilometre runs on a regular basis, you may find that you need to take in additional food to ensure you are

adequately fuelled for the duration of your run. At a higher training intensity (not the extremely slow joggers), your main fuel comes from carbohydrates, and you may find, in and around a training programme, that your carbohydrate requirements or intake will have to be increased. This can be done around training and/or at your meals. In choosing between these two options (meals/training), you should factor in your body composition goals and training times, etc. This is not, however, an excuse to eat more jelly babies/cake/sweets, since the quality of the carbohydrate still needs to be considered.

Once you are running 40 to 60 kilometres a week, you will need to eat more than an average 10-kilometre runner. You can easily meet this requirement by simply increasing the amount of what you are already eating, targeting your meals *and* your training: a little more chicken, an extra potato, more fruit, and the provision of extra snacks around training.

It is worth noting that, generally, women do not increase their intake enough when training – often due to multiple reasons. At a certain level of training (or energy expenditure), if you don't increase your food intake, your body will not train effectively and you may cause unnecessary imbalances in energy and micronutrients, leading to increased risk of poor recovery, injury, illness and, in extreme cases, bone density changes that could lead to stress fractures.

The (increased) need for carbohydrates should be in proportion to the duration and intensity of the exercise and to your physical size. During your training, this means there is quite a wide range for requirements – it could be anything from one banana for every extra 10 kilometres, to a jam sandwich and some raisins. The need may also be influenced by your body composition or training goals. For example, if you are starting with longer but slow, steady runs, it may be beneficial to take in less than you require or not to take in carbohydrates at all during this phase of your training, to promote increases in your fat-burning capacity (it is not advised to forgo fuel in your high-intensity sessions). This idea of carbohydrate or fuel periodisation (matching nutrition intake to your training session, both for fuel and recovery) is not new, but is often not well implemented without guidance.

Some people prefer to drink rather than eat, owing to lack of appetite or gut tolerance, and this is where sports drinks, or the more compact refined-food options can be useful. Note that it is possible to train your stomach and digestive system to increase its capacity for food/sports drink in a similar way to training your muscles to run further. Practically, start with small bites/sips and progress from there.

Train as you will race

Once you have started including regular longer runs as part of your training – for example, if you are doing 15- and 18-kilometre routes ahead of a half-marathon – you will want to eat on those long runs in the same way as you would plan on eating during your race.

Your intake during training may also depend on how much and what you eat before and after each run. It's a good idea to *start* your runs with adequate fuel stores, and to include an additional recovery snack of carbohydrates and protein for afterwards. Keep in mind that this does not cover your fluid intake, and that water should be consumed in regular sips as per your thirst. Pre-run breakfasts/snacks need to be big enough to fuel your run, but not too big or too rich in fibre to cause discomfort. Most runners like to stick to two or three consistent options that they trust and use regularly.

Once you extend past a half-marathon, having a nutrition plan for your races will become as important as remembering to take your shoes to the start line. On getting to a race such as Comrades, using the route map, you can even mark out your eating/drinking stops in line with your splits.

Recovery

Recovery post-run is often the most neglected adjustment in your nutrition plan. The primary role is to replenish your muscle carbohydrate stores and to provide some protein to facilitate muscle repair. The timing of this snack is more important if you have more than one exercise session in your day. A recovery snack could be a yoghurt-and-fruit smoothie. Once again, the size of this snack will depend on the same factors mentioned previously (training goals, intensity, duration, body size) but should not be neglected as you progress past a half-marathon to a marathon/ultramarathon programme.

Gels, bars, mixes, sports drinks and other sports foods

Advances in the types of sports foods available mean there are an increasingly wide variety of preparations to choose from. The most important consideration is your personal capacity and tolerance to consume the products, whether they are gels or sweets, energy bars or trail mixes, Coke or sports drinks. Some people can tolerate refined sugar or fructose, other people can't. It's best to experiment with varying tastes, flavours and textures, and with foods versus fluids on your training runs, to see what you prefer. If you have a second, try to get them to carry a wide selection of choices for you so that you can pick what you feel like ingesting at the time, and you can then use the official tables as options rather than as emergency fuelling stations. You can also experiment with different options in recovery.

Working out what works best for you will probably involve a lot of trial and error – and there *should* be trial and error, particularly when you make a big transition, like going up from a half-marathon to a marathon. The key is to have all these fuel options tried and tested by the time you get to your race day. You cannot run a marathon, or further, without a fuelling strategy that you know works.

Together with the amount of time you are on the road, your own performance goals might indicate what you want to take in, and when to take it in. A gel in the last stretch of a 21-kilometre race can provide a nice little boost when you really want to push the last five kilometres. If you're taking it easy, and hanging at the back of the running pack, you probably won't need this – maybe just a few sips of the 'colourful' water station drink that's provided, for thirst. (Please also refer to the piece later in this section on multi-vitamins and supplements.)

Ergogenic aids (substances that are proven to enhance performance) for speed or recovery, joint health or cramp prevention, are touted to runners all the time. However, in research, caffeine is one of very few substances that has been shown statistically (1%–3%) to improve performance. Commercial products now include caffeine as a result and may help you with that last dash to the finish. However, be aware that the timing (how long it takes for the caffeine to 'kick in') and the amount that you should include as part of your fuelling plan should also be tried and tested. Some runners may respond negatively to caffeine as it can amplify anxiety or the shakes pre-run.

It is important also to stress that the supplement industry is not regulated. Therefore, any recovery drink, muscle fuel, diet shake, etc.

has the risk of being contaminated with all sorts of unknown ingredients and its effects on health may not have been tested. Focusing on 'food first' is thus the golden rule.

Water and hydration

Learning how much fluid you need is an essential part of training. When you are thirsty, you should drink. If you are running in hotter weather, you will need to drink more. Some athletes lose up to three litres of body water during a marathon. Due to the motion of running, you might find it difficult to try to drink that much over the course of a race. Secondly, the dangers of over-drinking and possible hyponatremia (diluted sodium in the blood) are very real, especially for slower runners on colder days, and those with a predisposition to kidney issues. Due to these factors, women are often at higher risk of over-drinking. As a rule of thumb, you should never put on weight during the course of a run.

A sports drink can kill two birds with one stone: it offers an ideal way to get in fluid as well as carbohydrates at the same time, so is a practical during-a-run option. The sodium, albeit not a significant amount, may help with some of the absorption of what is in your gut. Bearing this in mind, palatability, temperature, the amount you drink, and the concentration of carbohydrates (sugars) and type of carbohydrate – for example, fructose vs maltodextrin – are quite important.

It is always important to start off a run as normally hydrated as possible, topping up by taking small sips of water at frequent intervals whilst running, and monitoring how much you drink. If you can, carry a bottle so you can reference your intake.

Multi-vitamins and supplements

There is, currently, no strong evidence that taking a multi-vitamin or supplement will improve your performance as a runner – if you are already well-nourished. If your own diet is adequate and varied enough, you will not need (nor benefit from) any additional nutritional supplements. The same applies to theories around taking calcium and magnesium to prevent exercise-associated cramps. Usually, cramping during exercise is strongly associated with fatigue – either because you are over-reaching, or because you are under-fuelled (for example, you over-train during a week, and don't fuel adequately before or during a run). If you suspect that your diet is not always ideal, a broad-spectrum, low-dose multi-vitamin is more appropriate than a high-dose single-nutrient supplement. There is evidence to show that higher doses of a single nutrient supplement can be as detrimental. When in doubt, a dietitian can assist.

Be aware of your self

In a world of everyone telling you what is good or not good for you, it is important to try to sift through the mountains of nutritional information available in the media. With self-awareness and monitoring, you can approach any new information appropriately. Monitoring over time can allow you to identify issues early on.

If you find that you are losing or gaining weight, that you are tired all the time, that you are not recovering well, or you are not sleeping properly, these are all possible indications you are not adjusting your intake correctly, and that you've missed something in your eating plan (either eating too much, too little, or something else). Developing an awareness of what your body is telling you allows you to notice these changes, and assess or re-assess your intake.

Some of the common running complaints involve:
- Fatigue
- Increased/decreased appetite
- Sore muscles (poor recovery)
- Nausea during races
- Other GIT (gastrointestinal tract) complaints on longer events.

These complaints can all be addressed with a strategic plan, worked out in collaboration with a dietitian. Even if you are thinking of taking a specific supplement, it may be money better spent seeing a dietitian, to see if it is really needed.

Final points to write on the fridge
- Support your training with good nutrition
- Discover your own needs through trial and error
- Never try anything new on race day.

Running Safety and Etiquette
Nechama Brodie

Taking up running comes with its own 'Rules of the Road'. Some of these 'rules' are simply about being polite, which is never a bad thing, but these guidelines will also make you a safer runner – again, not only for your own benefit, but for the safety of other runners (and cyclists, and even car and bike drivers) who are on the road.

1. Wear highly visible clothing
Black may be the most slimming colour, but it makes it harder for motorists to spot you. If you're on an uncontrolled road area (that is, not during a race, when streets are blocked off and vehicle traffic is controlled by marshalls), make sure you wear at least one large item of clothing that is highly visible against the tar or pavement. This might be a white or bright-coloured vest, shorts or running tights, or a reflective belt or vest.

2. Never assume that motor vehicle drivers have spotted you
Even if you are wearing luminous clothing and lit up like a Christmas tree, never assume that the driver of a car (or bike or truck) has seen you. When runners play games of Chicken with drivers, it's always the runner who loses. Pay particular attention to cars that seem to be driving erratically. Sadly, drunk and inattentive drivers still cause regular deaths (of runners, cyclists and pedestrians) each year.

3. Don't run more than two people abreast

When you're running with friends or your running club, never run more than two people abreast – unless it's during a race and the road is blocked off and vehicle traffic is controlled. When runners intrude too far into the road it's an immediate safety hazard. And, as above, in a game of car vs human, the car will win. If your route takes you along roads where there is a very narrow shoulder, drop down to single file.

4. Safety in numbers

As with point 2, running with a group is no guarantee that you will be spotted by an inattentive or impaired driver – but groups of runners are (generally, but not always) less likely to be targeted for random crimes, such as muggings, than lone runners. This is particularly important if you're running through areas that you don't know very well, or if your route takes you through public parks and green spaces.

5. Ditch the headphones

Music can be a great way to get you moving – and even help you push through the really hard parts of your race – but, when you're on the open road, it can also be a liability. While you're grooving to your favourite track, you might not hear the noise of an approaching car (or an approaching thug). During races, where the road environment is more controlled, if you do want to run with headphones/music, make sure the sound is turned down low enough so you can hear other runners – asking to pass, for example – and any route or safety officials who might be trying to communicate with you.

6. Say hello

One of the best parts about being a runner is discovering how friendly other runners can be. It's good form to greet other runners as you pass them (whether overtaking or coming in the opposite direction). If you're struggling up a steep hill, even a grunt of acknowledgement will do – and you'll probably be rewarded with not just a hello, but an encouragement to keep pushing on. For best results, greet the pedestrians you pass, and even the cyclists (although the latter might not always return the favour). Sharing a greeting only adds to the warm fuzzy feeling you'll get from having put in your run.

7. Race etiquette

How you behave on race day can have a direct impact on how other runners are able to enjoy their own run. Running might be a solo endeavour but, on race days, you're part of a mini-community. The more you look out for those around you, the more you can expect the same courtesies to be extended to you.

❏ *Don't push.* If you were an elite runner, you'd be at the head of the pack. If you're stuck in a pen with the majority, keep it contained. The same applies after the start gun has gone and you're working your way through the congestion that is typical of the first few kilometres. Pushing other runners because you're looking for a 10-second advantage on a non-elite-level time is bad form, creates bad vibes and can cause other runners to trip and injure themselves.
❏ *Let the slower runners ahead of you know that you want to come through.* If you need to dart through a small gap in order to pass through a congested group of runners, it's polite to let others know. You can say 'Excuse me' or 'May I pass?' or anything that alerts the

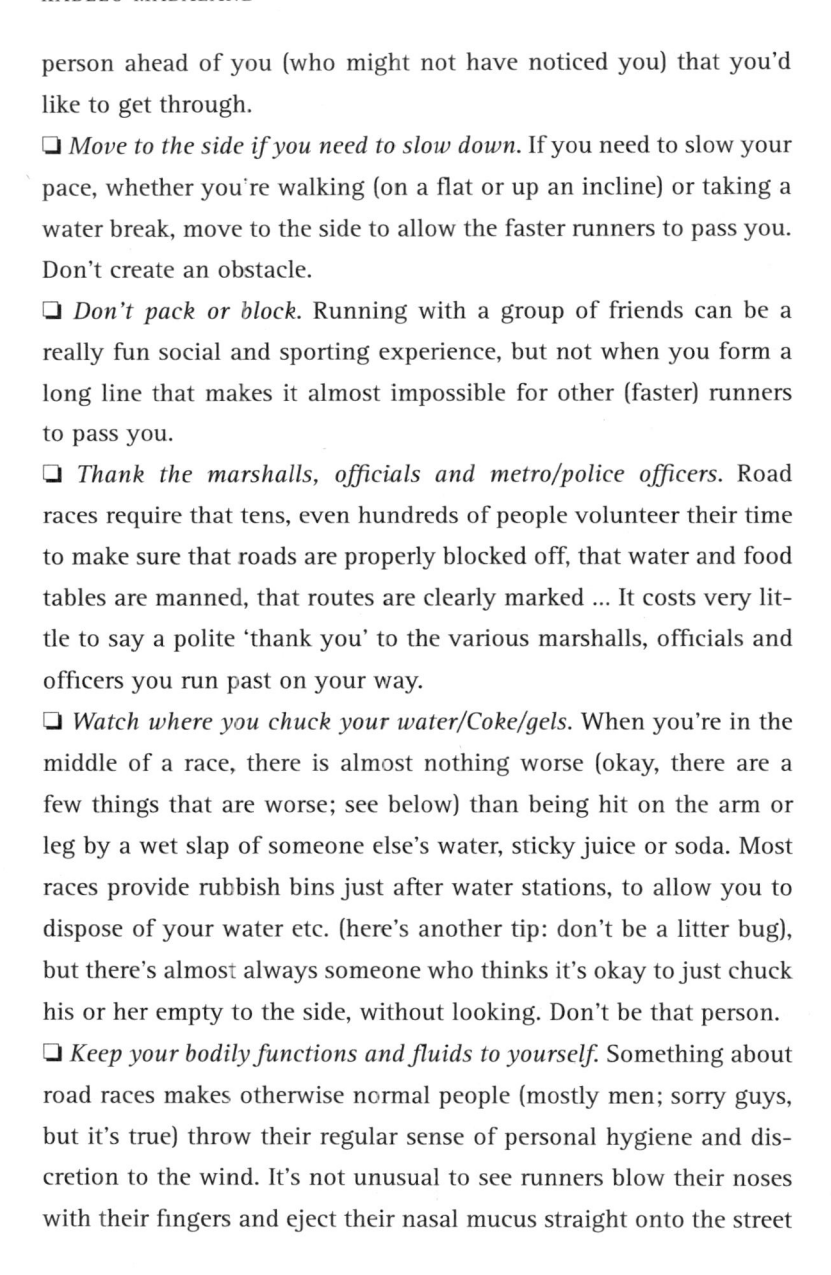

person ahead of you (who might not have noticed you) that you'd like to get through.

❏ *Move to the side if you need to slow down.* If you need to slow your pace, whether you're walking (on a flat or up an incline) or taking a water break, move to the side to allow the faster runners to pass you. Don't create an obstacle.

❏ *Don't pack or block.* Running with a group of friends can be a really fun social and sporting experience, but not when you form a long line that makes it almost impossible for other (faster) runners to pass you.

❏ *Thank the marshalls, officials and metro/police officers.* Road races require that tens, even hundreds of people volunteer their time to make sure that roads are properly blocked off, that water and food tables are manned, that routes are clearly marked ... It costs very little to say a polite 'thank you' to the various marshalls, officials and officers you run past on your way.

❏ *Watch where you chuck your water/Coke/gels.* When you're in the middle of a race, there is almost nothing worse (okay, there are a few things that are worse; see below) than being hit on the arm or leg by a wet slap of someone else's water, sticky juice or soda. Most races provide rubbish bins just after water stations, to allow you to dispose of your water etc. (here's another tip: don't be a litter bug), but there's almost always someone who thinks it's okay to just chuck his or her empty to the side, without looking. Don't be that person.

❏ *Keep your bodily functions and fluids to yourself.* Something about road races makes otherwise normal people (mostly men; sorry guys, but it's true) throw their regular sense of personal hygiene and discretion to the wind. It's not unusual to see runners blow their noses with their fingers and eject their nasal mucus straight onto the street (this, by the way, is worse than getting hit by a wet glob of Coke). Male runners – who have the advantage of being able to take a pee break almost anywhere – are politely requested to at least do so slightly out of sight of all the other runners.

Kabelo's Top Running Playlist

'Fly Away' by Lenny Kravitz
'*Khona*' by Mafikizolo
'Empire State of Mind' by Jay Z featuring Alicia Keys
'[...] Don't Kill My Vibe' by Kendrick Lamar
'Are You Gonna Go My Way' by Lenny Kravitz
'*Ndlovu Yangena*' by Tokollo
'No More Hunger' by Khuli Chana
'Victory Lap' by AKA
'*Gata Le Nna*' by JR
'*Viva La Vida*' by Coldplay
'Gust of Wind' by Pharrell Williams

Acknowledgements

This book was something of an ultramarathon on its own, fuelled by frequent cups of coffee instead of energy gels and shakes. While we got lost in conversations about life, family, music and meaning, the team at Pan Macmillan made sure we always had a warm, safe, private space to turn spoken words into written ones – and they guided us both on and off the page. To Terry Morris, Andrea Nattrass and Babongile Zulu, you were the greatest cheerleaders and the very best seconds to have on this journey!

We would also like to thank Ross Tucker, Lindsey Parry, Sarah Chantler and Shelly Meltzer for sharing their knowledge so generously, and helping us to develop and work through the excellent running plans and nutrition advice included in this book.

Finally, to each and every runner who finds the spirit to wake up long before the sun rises, who puts in the hard yards after a long working day, who looks at the uphill in front of them and tells themselves they're going to just do it ... However far you've come, however far you want to go, this book is for you.

– *Kabelo & Nechama*